DRAMATIC PROPHECIES
OF ELLEN WHITE

STORIES OF
WORLD EVENTS
DIVINELY
FORETOLD

HERBERT EDGAR DOUGLASS

Pacific Press® Publishing Association
Nampa, Idaho
Oshawa, Ontario, Canada
www.pacificpress.com

Cover design by Michelle C. Petz
Cover design resources from iStockphoto.com
Inside design by Steve Lanto

Unless otherwise noted, all Scripture quotations are from the New King James Version of the Bible, copyright © 1979, 1980, 1982, Thomas Nelson, Inc., Publishers.

The author is responsible for the accuracy of quotations and referenced material.

Additional copies of this book are available by calling toll free 1-800-765-6955 or by visiting http://www.adventistbookcenter.com.

Library of Congress Cataloging-in-Publication Data
Douglass, Herbert E.
Dramatic prophecies of Ellen White : stories of world events divinely
foretold / Herbert Edgar Douglass.
p. cm.
Includes bibliographical references.
ISBN 13: 978-0-8163-2192-6
ISBN 10: 0-8163-2192-2
1. White, Ellen Gould Harmon, 1827-1915—Prophecies. I. Title.
BX6193.W5D67 2007
286.7092—dc22
2006052171

08 09 10 11 • 5 4 3 2

DEDICATION

To Ellen White's great-grandson, Oliver Jacques, who has given his lifetime to fulfilling some of his "grandmother's" counsel: a missionary in Africa, a pastor/evangelist in America, chaplain at Battle Creek Sanitarium, longtime director of University Relations at Loma Linda University, and Vice President for Development at Kettering Medical Center.

CONTENTS

FOREWORD

This book should carry a warning: "Do not open unless you have time to read it from cover to cover!"

I speak from experience. I opened it with the thought that I would sample a few chapters. But when I finished chapter 1, I was "hooked." I read on and on, until suddenly (or so it seemed) I was into chapter 8. And, as the saying goes, "The rest is history."

What makes this book of special value during these bewildering times? Through concrete examples, it demonstrates that God is indeed in charge of world affairs. He declares "the end from the beginning, and from ancient times the things that are not yet done" (Isaiah 46:10). He is never caught by surprise. And in His love for His people He often reveals the future through His inspired messengers (see Amos 3:7). This is wonderfully reassuring—especially in times like these.

With consummate skill Dr. Douglass tells of future events that were revealed to Ellen White in vision. He also puts these forecasts in context. In some cases he shows how strange they must have sounded at the time they were given, but how up-to-the-minute they sound in this end time. Two striking examples are the rise of the United States to superpower status and the rise of the papacy to eminent international influence. The United States was but a fledgling nation when its world leadership role was forecast, and the Roman Catholic Church was in a weakened state, crippled by France, and a virtual fugitive.

Most readers will find chapter 2 a real eye-opener. They will be startled to learn that spiritualism in various forms—all designed to deceive—has become a major player in world affairs. Heads of state often seek counsel from the spirit world before making major decisions. And Christian churches—both Catholic and Protestant—are unwitting partners with spiritualism because of their shared belief that the soul is immortal. The groundwork is being laid for Satan's final deception that will unite the entire world against the people of God—Satan impersonating Christ. As the author of this book states, "It will be a time when one's future absolutely will hang on believing the Word of the Lord and the counsel of His last-day messenger, Ellen White."

Chapter 6 features the visions that embedded the great controversy theme in Mrs. White's writings. It is one of the most important chapters in the book, for it helps place in context not only the events in the other chapters of this book but the counsels Ellen White offers in her writings regarding education, health, theology, and business. The great controversy between Christ and Satan began in heaven but has affected all aspects of life in our world ever since Adam and Eve sinned in the Garden of Eden. It involves every nation, every church, every community, every individual. God is winsomely telling His side of the story, offering salvation, while Satan is deceiving and demonstrating the results of following his principles. This chapter is worth the price of the book.

Few writers can match Dr. Douglass's literary skill in selecting historical events of prophetic significance and packaging them so that readers will feel their relevance to one's personal faith. As with his other writings, this volume strengthens faith, builds confidence in God's last-day messenger, and leads one to borrow the language of the apostle Peter when he exclaimed, "We have not followed cunningly devised fables" (2 Peter 1:16).

Kenneth H. Wood
Chair, Ellen G. White Estate
Silver Spring, Maryland
November 21, 2006

Chapter One

A Most Stunning Prediction—The American Civil War

Ellen White's Civil War visions were perhaps the most stunning of her many predictions. In the sense that horrific calamities so quickly validated her forecasts—made many months before anyone else foresaw what she saw in vision—these visions were certainly among the most dramatic and impressive insights into the future that God gave her.

Her first Civil War vision, lasting twenty minutes, occurred during an afternoon church service in Parkville, Michigan, about thirty miles south of Battle Creek, on January 12, 1861. Ellen was thirty-three years old. The summer before, J. N. Loughborough and J. N. Andrews had held an evangelistic meeting in Parkville and erected a church building.

Following the morning sermon by J. H. Waggoner, Ellen gave what was reported as a "very powerful exhortation." After returning to her seat, she had a vision that lasted for at least twenty minutes. When breathing returned, she spoke briefly about the terrors of the coming war. At that time very few in the United States were antici-pating a long or bloody affair. Some of what she reported when she came out of vision related directly to several individuals and families in the audience.

Her words made a lasting impression on the young conference evangelist J. N. Loughborough, who recorded Ellen's words: "There is not a person in this house who has even dreamed of the trouble that is coming upon this land. People are making sport of the secession ordinance of South Carolina, but I have just been shown that a large number of States are going to join that State, and there will be a most terrible war."[1]

First vision three months before war began

Remember, this vision was given on January 12, 1861, three months before war began on April 12, 1861. In mid-February, Thomas Cobb from Georgia, while preparing the Confederate constitution, said, "The almost universal belief here is that we shall not have war."[2] Two days before his inaugural address on March 4, 1861, Abraham Lincoln declared in Philadelphia, "I have felt all the while justified in concluding that the crisis, the panic, the anxiety of the country at this time is artificial."

Alexander H. Stephens, vice president of the Confederacy, told a Savannah, Georgia, audience on March 21, 1861, that the southern revolution had thus far been accomplished "without shedding a drop of blood" and that the fear of a deadly collision with the Union was "nearly dispelled."

Now, back to Ellen's description of her vision:

In this vision I have seen large armies of both sides gathered on the field of battle. I heard the booming of the cannon, and saw the dead and dying on every hand. Then I saw them rushing up engaged in hand-to-hand fighting [bayoneting one another]. Then I saw the field after the battle, all covered with the dead and dying. Then I was carried to prisons, and saw the sufferings of those in want, who were wasting away. Then I was taken to the homes of those who had lost husbands, sons, or brothers in the war. I saw there distress and anguish.[3]

Then, looking over the congregation, Ellen White added, "There are those in this house who will lose sons in that war."

There is an interesting sidelight to this vision: A physician, who was also a spiritualist medium, was in the congregation that day. He had heard of Mrs. White and her visions and boasted that if ever he were present when she was in vision, he could bring her out of it in a minute. While she was in vision that day, James White explained her condition and gave an opportunity for those who wished to examine her to do so.

Someone near the back of the room was heard to say, "Doctor, go ahead and do what you said you would." James White, knowing nothing of the physician's boast, invited him to come forward and examine Mrs. White.

The doctor moved forward boldly, then stopped suddenly. James White stepped down, went to the man, and put his hand on his shoulder, urging him to come closer to Ellen. The physician carefully checked her pulse, her heartbeat, and what should have been her breathing. In startled tones, he declared, "Elder, her heart and pulse are all right, but there is not any breath in her body!"

Pulling away rather quickly, he made a beeline for the church door. Those near the door blocked his exit and said to him, "Go back, and bring her out of vision as you said you would." James White, taking the whole thing in, called upon the physician to report to the whole audience the result of his examination. Those close to him asked, "Doctor, what is it?"

"God only knows," he replied. "Let me out of this house." And he fled.[4]

Judge Osborne, the local judge, was also at the meeting. His wife was a seventh-day Sabbath keeper. The judge told Loughborough, "It was evident to all of us that the spirit that controlled the doctor as a medium and the Spirit that controlled Mrs. White in vision had no sympathy with each other." By the judge's side sat Mr. Shelhouse, owner of a large woolen mill. His father was elder of the Adventist church in Colon, about six miles away. These two men looked at Loughborough and shook their heads when Mrs. White told them what was coming. Little did they realize what she meant when she said that some "in this house will lose sons in that war."

Second Civil War vision

The next vision concerning the Civil War occurred at Roosevelt, New York, on the weekend of August 3 and 4. After James White gave a short talk, Ellen also spoke briefly, and then she was taken off into a vision that lasted about ten to fifteen minutes. Of this vision Ellen White wrote,

At the Conference at Roosevelt, New York, August 3, 1861 . . . I was taken off in vision and shown the sin of slavery, which has so long been a curse to this nation. . . . God's scourge is now upon the North, because they have so long submitted to the advances of the slave power. The sin of Northern proslavery men is great. They have strengthened the South in their sin by sanctioning the extension of slavery; they have acted a prominent part in bringing the nation into its present distressed condition.

I was shown that many do not realize the extent of the evil which has come upon us. They have flattered themselves that the national difficulties would soon be settled and confusion and war end; but all will be convinced that there is more reality in the matter than was anticipated. Many have looked for the North to strike a blow and end the controversy. . . .

All the abuse and cruelty exercised toward the slave is justly chargeable to the upholders of the slave system, whether they be Southern or Northern men.

The North and the South were presented before me. The North have been deceived in regard to the South. They [the

South] are better prepared for war than has been represented. Most of their men are well skilled in the use of arms, some of them from experience in battle, others from habitual sporting. . . .

I had a view of the disastrous battle at Manassas, Virginia. It was a most exciting, distressing scene. The Southern army had everything in their favor and were prepared for a dreadful contest. The Northern army was moving on with triumph, not doubting but that they would be victorious. Many were reckless and marched forward boastingly, as though victory were already theirs. As they neared the battlefield, many were almost fainting through weariness and want of refreshment. They did not expect so fierce an encounter. They rushed into battle and fought bravely, desperately. The dead and dying were on every side. Both the North and the South suffered severely. The Southern men felt the battle, and in a little while would have been driven back still further. The Northern men were rushing on, although their destruction was very great. Just then an angel descended and waved his hand backward. Instantly there was confusion in the ranks. It appeared to the Northern men that their troops were retreating, when it was not so in reality, and a precipitate retreat commenced. This seemed wonderful to me.

Then it was explained that God had this nation in His own hand, and would not suffer victories to be gained faster than He ordained, and would permit no more losses to the Northern men than in His wisdom He saw fit, to punish them for their sins. And had the Northern army at this time pushed the battle still further in their fainting, exhausted condition, the far greater struggle and destruction which awaited them would have caused great triumph in the South. God would not permit this, and sent an angel to interfere. The sudden falling back of the Northern troops is a mystery to all. They know not that God's hand was in the matter.

The destruction of the Southern army was so great that they had no heart to boast. The sight of the dead, the dying, and the wounded gave them but little courage to triumph. This destruction, occurring when they had every advantage, and the North great disadvantage, caused them much perplexity. They know that if the North have an equal chance with them, victory is certain for the North. Their only hope is to occupy positions difficult of approach, and then have formidable arrangements to hurl destruction on every hand.

The South have strengthened themselves greatly since their rebellion first commenced. If active measures had then been taken by the North, this rebellion would have been speedily crushed out. But that which was small at first has increased in strength and numbers until it has become most powerful. Other nations are intently watching this nation, for what purpose I was not informed, and are making great preparations for some event. The greatest perplexity and anxiety now exists among our national men. Proslavery men and traitors are in the very midst of them; and while these are professedly in favor of the Union, they have an influence in making decisions, some of which even favor the South.[5]

When I think of Mrs. White's dire warnings and vivid descriptions of horrible casualties in forthcoming Civil War battles, I am immediately drawn to her validation by eyewitnesses. General U. S. Grant's *Memoirs* includes this account of the large numbers of casualties:

This [building] had been taken as a hospital, and all night wounded men were brought in, their wounds dressed, a leg or an arm amputated as the case might require, and everything being done to save life or alleviate suffering. The sight was more unendurable than encountering the enemy's fire, and I returned to my tree in the rain.

I saw an open field, in our possession on the second day, over which the Confederates had made repeated charges the day before, so covered with dead that it would have been possible to walk across the clearing, in any direction stepping on dead bodies, without a foot touching the ground.[6]

What the rest of the country was saying

From all accounts, no one in the world in the early part of 1861 had such a preview of the Civil War as Ellen White. *The existing record of newspapers and speeches from the first half of 1861 were saying just the opposite of what was being shown to her in vision.*

For example, note these quotations from contemporary sources:

Let us make quick work. . . . A strong, active "pull together" will do our work effectually in thirty days.[7]

If Abraham Lincoln is equal to the position he fills, this war will be over by January, 1862.[8]

It is now recommended that you give legal means for making this contest a short and decisive one.[9]

Whatever war there is, may easily be made a war at sea,—a war of blockades,—a war having for its sole object the protection of American property and preservation of American commerce.[10]

Like everyone, [Lincoln] cherished a hope that powerful advances in Virginia and down the Mississippi would end the fighting in 1862.[11]

But the war went on, and on. The cost? The *Encyclopaedia Britannica* estimates that the Civil War cost "a total of some $11,450,500,000 for the North alone. But the cost to the South was enormous; $4,000,000,000 cannot be an exaggeration. It follows that, up to 1909, the cost of the war to the nation had approximated the tremendous total of $15,500,000,000 . . . and the death of probably 300,000 men on each side."[12]

In the fall of 1861, General William Sherman pressed Simon Cameron, U. S. Secretary of War, for 60,000 troops immediately and an additional 200,000 to meet future demands. Although this came nine months after Ellen White's Parkville vision, Sherman was criticized by the press as mentally unbalanced. One month after this request, General Henry Halleck relieved Sherman of his command. But in the next four years, both Ellen White and General Sherman were proved to be realists.[13]

That Parkville vision

You may be wondering about that prediction of sons being lost that Ellen White gave at the Parkville, Michigan, church before hostilities began. About a year later, Elder Loughborough returned to Parkville to speak. Judge Osborne and Mr. Shelhouse again sat together in the same seats as earlier. Elder Loughborough spoke on spiritual gifts and used Ellen White as his illustration. He referred to the vision of January 12, 1861. But there was no shaking of heads by these two men this time. Instead, their faces were in their handkerchiefs, sobbing bitter tears. One had lost his only son in the war; the other had lost a son on a different battlefield and had another son who was at that time a prisoner of war in the South.

The local elder was able to recall immediately the names of five families in the Parkville church who had lost sons in the fighting and said that, if given a little time, he could probably list five more families whose sons had been killed. This story we tell today in the restored

Parkville church that was moved forty miles to the Historic Adventist Village in Battle Creek. To sit today in that church and reflect on how God worked through His messenger is a sobering and faith-building experience. Can there be any doubt that we have a sure word of prophecy in the ministry of Ellen White?

1. J. N. Loughborough, *The Rise and Progress of Seventh-day Adventists* (Battle Creek, Mich.: General Conference Association of the Seventh-day Adventists, 1892), 236.

2. I am indebted to Lee Ellsworth Eusey and his master of arts thesis, "The American Civil War: An Interpretation," Andrews University, April 1965, for these quotations concerning attitudes toward the impending clash between the North and South. A more complete listing will be found in Appendix O in my book *Messenger of the Lord.*

3. Loughborough, *Rise and Progress,* 236, 237.

4. Arthur L. White, *Ellen G. White: The Early Years* (Washington, D.C.: Review and Herald® Publishing Association, 1985), 464.

5. Ellen G. White, *Testimonies for the Church* (Mountain View, Calif.: Pacific Press® Publishing Association, 1948), 1:264–268.

6. *Personal Memoirs of U. S. Grant* (New York: Charles L. Webster Co., 1885–1886), 1:349, 356.

7. *New York Times* editorial, around May 1, 1861, quoted in Robert L. Dabney, *Life and Campaigns of Thomas J. Jackson* (New York: Blelock and Co., 1866), 210 n.

8. *Harper's Weekly,* May 4, 1861.

9. Abraham Lincoln, in a letter to Congress, July 4, 1861, cited in Carl Sandberg, *Abraham Lincoln, The War Years* (New York: Charles Scribner's Sons, 1939), 3:290.

10. Editorial, *New York Times,* January 10, 1861.

11. Allan Nevins, *War for the Union* (New York: Charles Scribner's Sons, 1959), 2–5.

12. "Civil War" *Encyclopaedia Britannica,* 11th ed.

13. See William T. Sherman, *Memoirs of General William T. Sherman* (New York: Appleton and Co., 1876), 1:203–205, 217.

Chapter Two

THE RISE OF SPIRITUALISM—WHY WE CAN'T ALWAYS BELIEVE OUR EYES OR EARS

In 1848, Ellen White was twenty-one years old. For the past three years she had come in contact with individuals who had experienced and who were promoting various kinds of spiritism ranging from mesmerism to trances to apparent "miracles." In fact, the rampant growth of spiritist groups, including the Shakers, prompted the Millerite leaders assembled at the Albany Conference in 1845 to vote the following resolution: "*Resolved,* That we have no confidence in any new messages, visions, dreams, tongues, miracles, extraordinary gifts, revelations, impressions, discerning of spirits, or teachings, etc., etc., not in accordance with the unadulterated word of God."[1]

Part of this resolution was aimed at the "spiritualists"[2] who continued to believe that the date 1844 was still valid and that Jesus had indeed come individually to the faithful, not physically but spiritually! Some of them, believing that they were now living in the millennium, claimed to be sinless and refused to work because doing so would deny their conviction that Jesus indeed had come. Some claimed "spiritual wives" while others embraced celibacy.

Young Ellen had to find her way through all this confusion and was often targeted herself as another of these self-appointed "spiritualistic" prophets. She wrote,

In the period of disappointment after the passing of the time in 1844, fanaticism in various forms arose. Some held that the resurrection of the righteous dead had already taken place. I was sent to bear a message to those believing this, as I am now bearing a message to you. They declared that they were perfected, that body, soul, and spirit were holy. They made demonstrations similar to those you have made, and confused their own minds and the minds of others by their wonderful suppositions. Yet these persons were our beloved brethren, and we were longing to help them. I went into their meetings. There was much excitement, with noise and confusion. One could not tell what was piped or what was harped. Some appeared to be in vision, and fell to the floor. Others were jumping, dancing, and shouting. They declared that as their flesh was purified, they were ready for translation. This they repeated again and again. I bore my testimony in the name of the Lord, placing His rebuke upon these manifestations.[3]

Regardless of her protests against these spiritualizers, Mrs. White was often misunderstood until other emerging Sabbatarian Adventists could make the distinction clearer. She noted, "I have frequently been falsely charged with teaching views peculiar to Spiritualism. But before the editor of the *Day-Star* ran into that delusion, the Lord gave me a view of the sad and desolating effects that would be produced upon the flock by him and others in teaching the spiritual views."[4]

Something happened in 1848 that changed everything

Though these isolated and local manifestations were distracting in the 1840s, something happened in 1848 that would dramatically change the future appeal of spiritualism—a thrust that would unfold beyond anyone's imagination in the mid-nineteenth century, an unfolding that would have profound implications in the end time.

Historians generally agree that the modern spiritualist movement began with the "knocking" or "rapping" on the walls of a home in Hydesville, New York, about thirty-five miles east of Rochester, the home of the Fox family. Two sisters, Kate and Margaret Fox, reported that they were frightened by a strange tapping or knocking on a wall, by bedclothes being pulled off the bed, and by furniture moving around the room. After controlling their fears, they devised a code by which they could communicate with the "knocker." Further research indicated that the sisters were communicating with the departed murdered "spirit" of Charles B. Rosna, killed in that home. What was extraordinary about this report was that "the spirit" communicated through physical "rappings," and not simply through a person in a trance. Thus modern spiritualism, claiming to "talk" with the spirits of those who had died, was born![5]

This unexpected development was far different from the odd behavior of previous self-styled spiritualists. No longer centered only in darkened rooms bathed in candlelight, spiritualism attracted prominent men and women, who became its advocates by pen and practice.

Behind all spiritualistic phenomena—the idea of an immortal soul

What is behind all this? One of the core reasons for this rising interest in modern-day spiritualism is the notion of the immortal soul, advocated by both Catholics and most Protestants. Without that false belief, spiritualism would not exist today. Probably not one in a million today realize that this idea entered the Christian church, not from biblical teachings, but straight out of Greek philosophy. But that is a topic for another book!

For sixty years, the writings of Emanuel Swedenborg and the teachings of Franz Mesmer provided support to those seeking personal knowledge of the afterlife. Swedenborg believed he could, in a trance state, "commune" with spirits, and his writings described the spirit world. Proclaiming that there is no heaven or hell, but rather a series of spheres through which the "departed spirit" ascends into higher levels of wisdom, Swedenborg taught that these "spirits" could mediate between God and humans.[6]

Mesmer did not deal in religious beliefs. Instead, he introduced a technique, later called mesmerism (often, hypnotism), that induced trances, in which the living could contact departed loved ones or spiritual beings in general.

These two streams of thought (Swedenborgianism and Mesmerism) combined in a strange American synthesis—modern spiritualism. Interestingly, this new movement provided one of the first forums for American women to speak to mixed audiences. At the same time, radical Quakers, campaigning for abolition and equal rights for women, created an impression in people's minds that helped put a "reform" stamp on the young spiritualist movement.

As one would guess, all this notoriety led to widespread fraud, leading to independent investigating commissions that repeatedly unmasked the trickery that lay behind many spiritualist activities. Nevertheless, something about spiritualism was attractive not only to the general public but also to a growing list of scientists and authors in America and elsewhere, including British author Arthur Conan Doyle, creator of Sherlock Holmes. Doyle contended that the constant focus on actual observation of phenomena kept English and American spiritualists from embracing the Eastern emphasis on reincarnation. Doyle is often called the "Saint Paul" of modern spiritualism.

Though disorganized, the movement spread throughout the world, but only in the United Kingdom did it become as popular as it was in the United States. American spiritualists would meet in private homes for séances, at lecture halls for trance lectures, at summer camps by the thousands—but spiritualism remained individualistic. In fact, for many years, medium and trance lecturers resisted any organization attempts!

Two forms

The movement took two forms: (1) physical phenomena, usually in private séances by means of raps, audible voices, or most often, materialized figures of departed loved ones; and (2) mental phenomena conveyed through the mind of a medium by clairvoyance, in which the medium "hears" the spirit, or by clairsentience, in which the medium senses the presence and thought of someone in the room.

Most spiritualists attend Christian churches. Within the Christian environment, spiritualists accept the same moral system, a belief in the Judeo-Christian God, mystical pantheism, Sunday services, and the singing of hymns. Along with these similarities, spiritualists believe that acts in this life do not lead the departed "spirit" into an eternity of heaven or hell but into constantly ascending spheres. Although they accept most biblical principles, they do not believe that the Bible is the primary source of knowledge, about either God or the afterlife.[7] Further, they believe that death is not a result of sin but is part of the divine purpose.

In the latter half of the twentieth century, spiritualism became increasingly syncretistic, embracing various forms of the New Age movement. In fact, there is much less interest today in the type of miraculous "materializing" mediumship that captivated Arthur Conan Doyle. Modern spiritualists prefer the term "survivalism." A wide audience watches their television channel, called the Psychic Friends Network.[8]

Ellen White's first vision regarding spiritualism

A few months after the phenomenon of the rappings at the Fox home in Hydeville, New York, was hitting the news, Ellen White received a vision at Topsham, Maine, on March 24, 1849. Describing the vision, she wrote, "I saw that the mysterious knocking in New York and other places, was the power of Satan; and that such things would be more and more common, clothed in a religious garb, to lull the deceived to more security; and to draw the minds of God's people, if possible, to those things and cause them to doubt the teachings, and power of the Holy Ghost."[9] And still later, she explained further: "The mysterious rapping with which modern spiritualism began was not the result of human trickery or cunning, but was the direct work of evil angels, who thus introduced one of the most successful of soul-destroying delusions. Many will be ensnared through the belief that spiritualism is a merely human imposture; when brought face to face with manifestations which they cannot but regard as supernatural, they will be deceived, and will be led to accept them as the great power of God."[10]

Thus she was shown early on that the mysterious rapping was in reality the work of evil angels, although many perceived it as the power of God, and that the phenomenon would fast spread beyond the Fox sisters, who now worked in traveling circuses and local vaudevilles.

And spread it did. Rapidly spiritualism was accepted in the Protestant and Catholic world because there was no doctrinal buffer in these religions to protect those beguiled by the undeniable manifestations of "mysterious" powers. Three major spiritualist churches exist today: the International General Assembly of Spiritualists, the National Spiritual Alliance of the U.S.A., and the National Spiritualist Association of Churches. Encyclopedias cover spiritualism as a religion—just as Ellen White predicted, even though not much evidence existed in her day for this remarkable growth.

Part of New Age thinking

Part of the amazing advance of New Age thought and practice is due to its claim to communicate with the dead. Channeling is one of the best-known features of New Age belief. Mesmerism, better known today as certain forms of hypnotism, is also a well-known element of spiritualistic philosophy. Along with Mesmer and Stefan Zweig, Swedenborg practiced bringing back messages from other spirits. These men believed that such powers added to the healing art—calling it "spirit healing by the entranced medium."

In recent years, spiritualism has contributed much to the New Age phenomenon. The New Age movement is a vague term for a collection of ideas derived from paganism combined with elements from both Eastern and Western religious traditions. One common thread linking all these ideas is the belief that spirituality is a very individual matter and that all people are, in some way, divine. Many New Agers believe in spiritual healing, channeling, ESP, dream interpretation, and other psychic phenomena as paths to develop spirituality by contacting spirits or getting in touch with one's past lives.

Ellen White's second vision on modern spiritualism

Ellen White received her second vision on modern spiritualism on March 24, 1849. She wrote on August 24, 1850,

> I saw that the "mysterious rapping" was the power of Satan; some of it was directly from him, and some indirectly, through his agents, but it all proceeded from Satan. It was his work that he accomplished in different ways; yet many in the churches and the world were so enveloped in gross darkness that they thought and held forth that it was the power of God. Said the angel, "Should not a people seek unto their God? for the living to the dead?" Should the living go to the dead for knowledge? The dead know not anything. For the living God do ye go to the dead? They have departed from the living God to converse with the dead who know not anything. See Isaiah 8:19, 20.
>
> I saw that soon it would be considered blasphemy to speak against the rapping, and that it would spread more and more, that Satan's power would increase and some of his devoted followers would have power to work miracles and even to bring

down fire from heaven in the sight of men. I was shown that by the rapping and mesmerism, these modern magicians would yet account for all the miracles wrought by our Lord Jesus Christ, and that many would believe that all the mighty works of the Son of God when on earth were accomplished by this same power.

I was pointed back to the time of Moses, and saw the signs and wonders which God wrought through him before Pharaoh, most of which were imitated by the magicians of Egypt; and that just before the final deliverance of the saints, God would work powerfully for His people, and these modern magicians would be permitted to imitate the work of God.[11]

I find these few, clear, unambiguous words to be astonishing, re-membering that they were written when followers of spiritualism were exceedingly few. Indeed, here Ellen White predicted that the time would come when any criticism of spiritualism would be charac-terized as "blasphemy."

A criminal act to speak against spiritualists?

Based on Ellen White's prediction, it would not surprise me for governments, in Western countries to begin with, to make it a crimi-nal act to speak against spiritualists. After all, laws are already on the books making it illegal to disparage anyone's ethnicity, sexual gen-der, or religious beliefs. As I write, Canadian judges are already imple-menting such laws against those who are only voicing their right to express their own religious beliefs. In the politically correct society in which we find ourselves today, we may be only a half-step away from being jailed for speaking against spiritualism.

Note this statement from 1948 Centennial Book of Modern Spiritual-ism: "Neither priest nor press should uncharitably speak of, or touch this holy word 'Spiritualism,' only with clean hands and pure hearts, and Spiritualists themselves should honor their blessed gospel of immortality."

Mrs. White predicted that specialists in extrasensory perception would recognize that these "mysterious powers" were far beyond the humanly devised tricks of a master magician. "Satan's power would increase," she wrote, and some of "his followers would have power to work miracles." Experiments today in numerous incidents of extrasensory perception validate that something is happening beyond human explanation.

In the *Encyclopedia Americana*, the founder of Duke University's Institute for Parapsychology wrote, "The question raised by Spiritualism must be faced as one of science's greatest problems."

The vision Ellen White received in 1850 on this topic zeroed in on two other aspects that then seemed incredible. The time would come, Ellen White said, when theologians and others would credit Christ's miracles to the powers of spiritualism. How accurate she was!

The second aspect was that in the last of the last days "God would work powerfully for His people, and these modern magicians [spiritualists] would be permitted to imitate the work of God."[12] Compare Revelation 13:13, 14.

The ultimate fraud

In 1854, Mrs. White elaborated on the counsel she had previously given regarding the rise of spiritualism:

> I saw the rapping delusion—what progress it was making, and that if it were possible it would deceive the very elect. Satan will have power to bring before us the appearance of forms purporting to be our relatives or friends now sleeping in Jesus. It will be made to appear as if these friends were present; the words that they uttered while here, with which we were familiar, will be spoken, and the same tone of voice that they had

while living will fall upon the ear. All this is to deceive the saints and ensnare them into the belief of this delusion.[13]

Here was added counsel to an emerging Adventist movement with a last-day assignment. Imagine having your "loved one" reappear, talking about matters that only he and you could possibly know. And then for the "loved one" to contradict such plain Bible truths as the atonement, the state of the dead, the seventh-day Sabbath, etc. Would it not be hard to think of a more subtle temptation?

Ellen White gave us clear instruction as to how to repel Satan's master plan to deceive the world in the end time:

I saw that the saints must get a thorough understanding of present truth, which they will be obliged to maintain from the Scriptures. They must understand the state of the dead; for the spirits of devils will yet appear to them, professing to be beloved friends and relatives, who will declare to them that the Sabbath has been changed, also other unscriptural doctrines. They will do all in their power to excite sympathy and will work miracles before them to confirm what they declare. The people of God must be prepared to withstand these spirits with the Bible truth that the dead know not anything, and that they who appear to them are the spirits of devils. Our minds must not be taken up with things around us, but must be occupied with the present truth and a preparation to give a reason of our hope with meekness and fear.[14]

The train with its conductor

Then Ellen White pictured a parable that has never left my mind since reading it more than sixty years ago. I think you will never forget it either:

I saw the rapidity with which this delusion was spreading. A train of cars was shown me, going with the speed of lightning. The angel bade me look carefully. I fixed my eyes upon the train. It seemed that the whole world was on board, that there could not be one left. Said the angel, "They are binding in bundles ready to burn." Then he showed me the conductor, who appeared like a stately, fair person, whom all the passengers looked up to and reverenced. I was perplexed and asked my attending angel who it was. He said, "It is Satan. He is the conductor in the form of an angel of light. He has taken the world captive. They are given over to strong delusions, to believe a lie, that they may be damned. This agent, the next highest in order to him, is the engineer, and other of his agents are employed in different offices as he may need them, and they are all going with lightning speed to perdition."

Ellen White continued,

I asked the angel if there were none left. He bade me look in an opposite direction, and I saw a little company traveling a narrow pathway. All seemed to be firmly united, bound together by the truth, in bundles, or companies. Said the angel, "The third angel is binding, or sealing, them in bundles for the heavenly garner." This little company looked careworn, as if they had passed through severe trials and conflicts. And it appeared as if the sun had just risen from behind a cloud and shone upon their countenances, causing them to look triumphant, as if their victories were nearly won.[15]

The rest of these pages in *Early Writings*, pages 87–91, contain additional counsel that you will not read anywhere else.

Awash in spiritualism today

Wherever we look today, we are awash in various forms of spiritualism, from the magazines at checkout stands in the local grocery to TV programs such as the January 1987 five-hour program, in which the American Broadcasting Company featured actress Shirley MacLaine's "personal trek through a psychic world." Amazing! But just another example of the accuracy of Ellen White's vision-based predictions.

Everywhere we look, we find more examples of Ellen White's vision-based predictions.[16] As I write, Allison DuBois, author of *Don't Kiss Them Good-bye* and her recently released *We Are Their Heaven,* is also famous for inspiring the NBC series *Medium,* starring Emmy-winning actress Patricia Arquette. Her story was featured in a two-page spread in the *Sacramento Bee*—a most remarkable recital of her lifelong connection with the dead. She has been tested by specialists in psychic phenomena, trying to prove to herself that her experiences were not purely subjective and without convincing evidence. The scientists' jaws dropped![17]

Another feature of the last few decades is the astounding fantasy game Dungeons and Dragons. But this attraction has morphed into even more sophisticated and cruel games such as RuneQuest, Chivalry & Sorcery, Arduin Grimoire, and Tunnels and Trolls, which are called fantasy role-playing games (FRPG). The players, mostly the young, identify with the characters, either good or bad. These games have been called the most magnificently packaged introduction to the occult in recorded history.[18]

Spiritual component in healing

Another phenomenon of the last fifty years has been the growing awareness in the medical community of the importance of the "spiritual" component of human beings—that the whole person needs treatment, not just the illness. Ellen White emphasized this spiritual component in much of her writings, especially in *The Ministry of Healing.*

But along with the good comes the counterfeit. Enter the spiritualist healer, one who is able to transmit curative energies and apply them to physical conditions—either through his or her own "inborn power" or through a medium. The results of spiritual healing are produced in several ways. One way is by spiritual influences working through the body of the medium to transmit curative energies to the diseased parts of the recipient's body. Another is by enlightening the mind of the medium through spiritual influences so that the cause, nature, and seat of the disease in the recipient is made known to the medium. The wide interest in TV healing by certain charismatic preachers dovetails with the healing aspects of modern spiritualism.

In her book, *The Great Controversy,* Ellen White included a chapter on spiritualism, ending with this forecast: "Little by little he [Satan] has prepared the way for his masterpiece of deception in the development of spiritualism. He has not yet reached the full accomplishment of his designs; but it will be reached in the last remnant of time. Says the prophet: 'I saw three unclean spirits like frogs; . . . they are the spirits of devils, working miracles, which go forth unto the kings of the earth and of the whole world, to gather them to the battle of that great day of God Almighty' (Revelation 16:13, 14)."[19]

In these few words we are looking at the final crescendo of the tsunami wave that began in Hydesville, New York, in 1849. Yet even today the world impact of spiritualism can scarcely be imagined!

End-time spiritualism

Let's follow Ellen White's vision-forecast of the end times. Note the picture she draws of the international impact of spiritualism:

> Fearful sights of a supernatural character will soon be revealed in the heavens, in token of the power of miracle-working

demons. The spirits of devils will go forth to the kings of the earth and to the whole world, to fasten them in deception, and urge them on to unite with Satan in his last struggle against the government of heaven. By these agencies, rulers and subjects will be alike deceived. Persons will arise pretending to be Christ Himself, and claiming the title and worship which belong to the world's Redeemer. They will perform wonderful miracles of healing and will profess to have revelations from heaven contradicting the testimony of the Scriptures.[20]

Not only will spiritualism be a uniting, cohesive manipulating force in end-time politics. The master spiritualist will personally enter the horrendous confusion that he, himself, has sponsored:

As the crowning act in the great drama of deception, Satan himself will personate Christ. The church has long professed to look to the Saviour's advent as the consummation of her hopes. Now the great deceiver will make it appear that Christ has come. In different parts of the earth, Satan will manifest himself among men as a majestic being of dazzling brightness, resembling the description of the Son of God given by John in the Revelation. Revelation 1:13-15. The glory that surrounds him is unsurpassed by anything that mortal eyes have yet beheld. The shout of triumph rings out upon the air: "Christ has come! Christ has come!" The people prostrate themselves in adoration before him, while he lifts up his hands and pronounces a blessing upon them, as Christ blessed His disciples when He was upon the earth. His voice is soft and subdued, yet full of melody. In gentle, compassionate tones he presents some of the same gracious, heavenly truths which the Saviour uttered; he heals the diseases of the people, and then, in his assumed character of Christ, he claims to have changed the Sabbath to Sunday, and commands all to hallow the day which he has blessed. He declares that those who persist in keeping holy the seventh day are blaspheming his name by refusing to listen to his angels sent to them with light and truth. This is the strong, almost overmastering delusion. . . .

But the people of God will not be misled. The teachings of this false christ are not in accordance with the Scriptures.[21]

God's early warning system on target

God's early warning system from 1849 through the 1880s sounded like a wild dream, a neurotic fantasy to those first reading or hearing these predictions. But we today have seen how rapidly "mysterious rappings" became a worldwide phenomenon. Once considered an object of interest in vaudeville, spiritualism soon became baptized, taking its place among Christian denominations. Chief among its "miracles" would be the "return" of dead loved ones, proving to many that spiritualism was more than magic. This notion of the immortality of the soul, coupled with the belief in extrasensory perceptions, is reflected in such activities as séances, Ouija boards, psychic powers, channeling, Wicca, out-of-body experiences, demonology, witchcraft, and astral projection.

I remember when *Embraced by the Light* spent many weeks on the *New York Times* best-seller list in 1993 through 1994. Why did Americans gobble it up? Because most people want assurance of life beyond the grave. Saturated with New Age notions, this book is the author's account of her "out of body experience," or as others call the phenomenon, "near death experience."

These tools of spiritism appeal to the sophisticated and learned as well as to the uneducated. Voodoo and its assorted witchcraft may captivate the uneducated, but channeling, out-of-body experiences, astral projection, even the Ouija board, fascinate the most educated individuals.

At the Naval Medical Center in Portsmouth, Virginia, Harris, a registered nurse, is also the "pagan resource" person—the one who is called upon "to offer spiritual aid to patients who describe themselves as witches, Wiccans, Odinists, or followers of other Earth-centered belief systems. . . . On behalf of pagan servicemen and servicewomen, Harris has handcrafted and consecrated healing talismans, cleansed hospital rooms of negative energy, and helped arrange healing rituals by covens."[22]

The appeal of spiritualism today

In a very instructive article in *Christianity Today*, Marvin Olasky, professor at the University of Texas (Austin), quotes historian Frank Podmore, in listing four major reasons for spiritism's appeal:

1. The ranks of the spiritualists were naturally recruited, largely from those who had freed themselves entirely from the Christian tradition, and had therewith lost all definite hope or belief in a future life.
2. Some flocked to spiritism because within it there was no real good or evil, and no sin. People could follow their "naturally benevolent instincts."
3. Spiritist showmanship was appealing.
4. Spiritism certainly appealed to those who had lost a spouse or child and hoped beyond hope to converse with the dead.

Olasky ends his article by saying that "those who try to syncretize New Age and Christian doctrines, either by proclaiming humanity's essential goodness or recommending 'visualization' techniques that place us at the center of things, should not be allowed to be church leaders."[23] It seems to me that he would have made his case stronger if he, himself, did not believe in an immortal soul!

In the end time, we can expect Satan's brilliance to dazzle the senses of all, the sophisticated and the less educated, in a way that has never yet been seen on this planet. "So closely will the counterfeit resemble the true that it will be impossible to distinguish between them except by the Holy Scriptures. By their testimony every statement and every miracle must be tested."[24] Why? Because impersonations of departed loved ones, astounding healings, shocking miracles of all kinds will overwhelm everyone who is not grounded in biblical truth.

Well-known leaders

Many faithful followers of spiritualism have also been well-known political leaders—such as William Lyon Mackenzie King, Canada's longest-serving prime minister. King was most pleased with what he considered to be communications with his mother, father, siblings, and famous contemporaries. In his June 30, 1932, diary, he wrote, "There can be no doubt whatsoever that the persons I have been talking with were the loved ones and others I have known and who have passed away. It was the spirits of the departed."

Another prominent leader who was also a spiritualist was Lord Dowding, commander of Great Britain's Royal Air Force (RAF) during the Battle of Britain. Through a medium friend, many of the dead airmen were able to give their former Chief convincing evidence of their "survival" beyond death. Lord Dowding would then pass on compassionate messages to the families of the dead airmen.

Who decided the exact time when President Reagan and Premier Gorbachev would sign the intermediate-range nuclear forces treaty? According to Time magazine's cover story "Astrology in the White House" (December 7, 1987), the astonishing answer seems to be the astrologer Joan Quigley, a Vassar graduate who has written three books on astrology.[25]

Donald Regan, the former White House Chief of Staff, has written,

> Virtually every major move or decision the Reagans made during my time as White House chief of staff was cleared in advance with a woman in San Francisco who drew up horoscopes to make certain that the planets were in a favorable alignment for the enterprise.[26]

First Lady Nancy Reagan dabbled in astrology as far back as 1967. Her trust in astrology, however, was bolstered in 1981 when Quigley showed her that the astrologer's chart predicted extreme danger for the President around March 30. On that date, John Hinckley severely wounded the President with a handgun. From that time on, Mrs. Reagan consistently consulted her astrologer to determine "propitious" times for her husband to travel, to make public appearances, and even to sign treaties.[27] A strange mixture of spirituality and superstition seems to be prevalent across the country!

No longer "fraudulent!"

In 1951, Great Britain passed the Fraudulent Mediums Act, repealing the Witchcraft Act of 1735. Spiritualists may now openly and legally practice their religion. Great Britain today has more than five hundred spiritualist churches.[28]

One of the many venues for spiritualistic gatherings is the Burning Man Festival, an annual six-day event held in the Black Rock Desert, 120 miles north of Reno, Nevada, the week prior to and including Labor Day weekend. In past years, the themes for the festival have included "Fertility," "Time," "Hell," "Outer Space," "The Body," "The Floating World," "Beyond Belief," "The Vault of Heaven," and "Psyche."

For 2006, the theme was "Hope and Fear." Recent attendance at The Burning Man Festival has surpassed 15,000 Wiccans, Satanists, goddesses (white witches), nudists, and a consortium of other party-goers who converge on the hot Nevada desert for a weekend of "glorious Hell on earth." The number of participants at the Burning Man gala has nearly doubled each year since 1986, and organizers hoped to break an attendance of 30,000 in 2006. The Burning Man is a no-holds-barred New Age "Woodstock" style festival, where neo-pagans, Wiccans, transvestite entertainers, and back-slidden Christians go to perform rituals, burn sacrifices to pagan gods and goddesses, dance in the nude, engage in sex, and otherwise "express" themselves and become one with Gaia (Mother Earth).

In the end time, spiritism will be the melding element that unites Protestants and Catholics. Again, why? Because both groups, with few exceptions, have bought Satan's lie regarding the immortal soul. Because of this common bond, it will be easier for these two groups to join together on other significant end-time issues, such as an international Sunday law.

The grand impersonator

But more than astounding miracles (which become only window-dressing), the real point and the grand finale of spiritualism's end-time scenario will be center stage—Satan himself appears impersonating Christ. After all the other "wonders" sponsored by spiritualism, why would anyone doubt this grand impersonation?

What is Ellen White's last word of counsel to us today as we face the stupendous climax to Satan's first lie and deception on planet Earth—the big lie that Eve fell for—"You will not surely die" (Genesis 3:4)?

Only those who have been diligent students of the Scriptures and who have received the love of the truth will be shielded from the powerful delusion that takes the world captive. By the Bible testimony these will detect the deceiver in his disguise. To all the testing time will come. By the sifting of temptation the genuine Christian will be revealed. Are the people of God now so firmly established upon His word that they would not yield to the evidence of their senses? Would they, in such a crisis, cling to the Bible and the Bible only? Satan will, if possible, prevent them from obtaining a preparation to stand in that day. He will so arrange affairs as to hedge up their way, entangle them with earthly treasures, cause them to carry a heavy, wearisome burden, that their hearts may be overcharged with the cares of this life and the day of trial may come upon them as a thief.[29]

Our only defense

Our only defense will be Bible truth in our minds, firmly in place through much study and sharing and personal commitment. We may have lived a lifetime believing only that which we have personally seen and experienced. But eyes and ears will not be a safe defense in the face of "undeniable evidence" that loved ones have reappeared, pleading with God's loyalists to forget their so-called biblical doctrines that now seem so divisive in a world seeking harmony and tolerance of everybody else's "religion."

The appeal of "departed" loved ones—*that we should really believe what we "see and hear"*—will be almost overwhelming, even to the most intelligent Bible student. It will be a time when one's future absolutely will hang on believing the Word of the Lord and the counsel of His last-day messenger, Ellen White.[30]

---

1. Quoted in Herbert E. Douglass, *Messenger of the Lord* (Nampa, Idaho: Pacific Press® Publishing Association, 1998), 37.

2. Not to be confused with what we think of as spiritualism today—those who believe they are communicating with the dead. Rather, in this context, "spiritualists" were those who insisted that Jesus *had* come in 1844, not physically, but spiritually to those with the insight to recognize the fact.

3. Ellen G. White, *Selected Messages*, vol. 2 (Washington, D.C.: Review and Herald® Publishing Association, 1958), 34.

4. Ellen G. White, *Early Writings* (Washington, D.C.: Review and Herald® Publishing Association, 1945), 77.

5. Kate and Margaret went on tour, promoting spiritualism. Other people joined them as mediums. In 1853, the first spiritualist church was founded and within two years, claimed to have two million followers.

6. Followers of Swedenborg have organized under the name "Church of New Jerusalem."

7. "Universal Spiritualism is the science, philosophy and religion of continuous life, based upon the demonstrated fact of communication, by means of spiritual channeling, with those who are in the spiritual world."—http://home.comcast.net/~spiritualism/Main/Main.html.

8. For many today, spiritualism is "scientific proof" of life after death, which doesn't involve any of the so-called nonsense of religion. In recent years, New Thought spiritualism seeks to promote the original intent of spiritualism that has been lost due to the focus on spirit communication over the development of spirituality. New Thought spiritualism denies the existence of any power or presence opposed to Infinite Intelligence. Evil and suffering are caused by man's ignorance. New Thought spiritualism does not have any creed; everyone has the right to his or her own beliefs. Everyone is a potential mystic, and spirit communication is a tool to help us understand the true nature of the universe and to help all to develop to the highest possible extent.

9. Ellen G. White, *Review and Herald*, August 1, 1849.

10. Ellen G. White, *The Great Controversy* (Nampa, Idaho: Pacific Press® Publishing Association, 1950), 553.

11. E. G. White, *Early Writings*, 59, 60.

12. Ibid., 60.

13. Ibid., 87.

14. Ibid.

15. Ibid., 88, 89.

16. Other examples include the Harry Potter phenomenon, and Marshall Applewhite, founder of the Heaven's Gate cult, whose thirty-nine members committed mass suicide in March 1997, believing they'd ascend to a spaceship hiding in the trail of the comet Hale-Bopp. They were inspired by the movie *Star Wars*.

17. *The Sacramento Bee,* June 19, 2006.

18. Gary North, *None Dare Call it Witchcraft* (New Rochelle, N.Y.: Arlington, House Publishers, 1976).

19. E. G. White, *The Great Controversy*, 561, 562.

20. Ibid., 624.

21. Ibid., 624, 625.

22. Associated Press, March 18, 2002.

23. *Christianity Today*, December 14, 1992. Between 1990 and 2001, the number of Wiccans has jumped 1,572 percent, from 8,000 to 134,000 self-proclaimed witches.—*USA TODAY*, December 24, 2001.

24. E. G. White, *The Great Controversy*, 593.

25. December 7, 1987.

26. Donald T. Regan, *Time*, May 16, 1988.

27. Barrett Seaman, *Time*, May 24, 1988.

28. Some affiliated with the Spiritualists National Church, others with Christian Spiritualist Union or the Greater World Christian Spiritualists Associations, plus many independent churches.

29. E. G. White, *The Great Controversy*, 625, 626.

30. For further reading, see Douglass, *Messenger of the Lord,* 37, 160; A. L. White, *The Early Years*, 188 (see chap. 1, n. 4).

Chapter Three

MISUNDERSTOOD BY MANY—MEASURED COUNSEL REGARDING THE COLOR LINE

One of the most difficult and long-lasting social problems in the United States has been the black/white tension. So much horror, so much misunderstanding! For many, the problem still lingers.

For the Seventh-day Adventist Church, the voice of Ellen G. White has been the most instructive, most steadying influence in this area. Problems of race still exist in the church today, but without her counsel, the Adventist Church would have fumbled miserably throughout the twentieth century in dealing with the color line. She saved the Adventist Church from profound embarrassment, on one hand, and from dreadful, appalling conflict, on the other. Troubles? Yes! But nothing like what might have been!

When we review Ellen White's counsel regarding racial issues in the years following the Civil War up to the years just prior to her death in 1915, we see insight, wisdom, and courage—even when she was misunderstood. She never buckled under pressure over race relations.

"Not to live or die a coward"

On March 21, 1891, Ellen White spoke to thirty church leaders gathered at the General Conference session at Battle Creek, Michigan, on the subject "Our Duty to the Colored People." She said,

> I know that which I now speak will bring me into conflict. This I do not covet, for the conflict has seemed to be continuous of late years; *but I do not mean to live a coward or die a coward, leaving my work undone.* I must follow in my Master's footsteps. . . . The God of the white man is the God of the black man, and the Lord declares that His love for the least of His children exceeds that of a mother for her beloved child. . . . The Lord's eye is upon all His creatures; He loves them all, and makes no difference between white and black, except that He has a special, tender pity for those who are called to bear a greater burden than others. . . . The ignorant and the wise, the rich and the poor, the heathen and the slave, white or black—Jesus paid the purchase money for their souls. If they believe on Him, His cleansing blood is applied to them. The black man's name is written in the book of life beside the white man's. All are one in Christ. Birth, station, nationality, or color cannot elevate or degrade men. The character makes the man.[1]

Misunderstood by many

In this area, why has Ellen White been misunderstood by some, especially since her death in 1915? There are two reasons.

First, some of her counsel was written during the sad period of what has been called the Reconstruction of the South. The blacks were betrayed. Segregation had settled in and was accepted by the majority of white people, North and South. Wise counsel given by Mrs. White during this appalling period seemed to conflict with her counsel given before segregation became so ruthless. When we look at her counsel in terms of the *existing circumstances* when she wrote, we get a clear understanding of her deep and caring insights. The principle of considering time, place, and circumstances is the *only* guideline that we can use today to understand any writer—especially Ellen White, who spoke with careful consideration.

Second, not all her counsel on this topic was easily available even decades after it was written. Church members in general did not have ready access to articles in older issues of the church paper, the *Review and Herald*. A most helpful small book, *The Southern Work*, containing many Ellen White letters and other materials not otherwise available, had been published in 1898 but went out of print and seems to have been forgotten until it was republished in 1966. In other words, a more complete picture of the black ordeal within the nation and the church in the late 1800s and early 1900s and Ellen White's counsel regarding the situation was not readily at hand for many decades prior to 1966. Of course, in recent years the CD-ROM has brought all her counsel together in one place and is now available through the E. G. White Estate.

What *was* in print were pages in *Testimonies for the Church*, volume 9, that would have been understood clearly when they were first written in the late 1890s and the early 1900s. However, in later years, when *stripped of historical context*, the words sounded harsh. Unfortunately, wise policies meant for the moment became understood as principles that were to be for all time to come. Not a good situation!

Misunderstood statements in *Testimonies*, volume 9

- Cautions were sent that every movement must be guarded, that the workers were to make no political speeches, and that the mingling of whites and blacks in social equality was by no means to be encouraged.[2]
- Let as little as possible be said about the color line, and let the colored people work chiefly for those of their own race.

  In regard to white and colored people worshiping in the same building, this cannot be followed as a general custom with profit to either party—especially in the South. The best thing will be to provide the colored people who accept the truth, with places of worship of their own, in which they can carry on their services by themselves.[3]

- Let the colored believers have their place of worship and the white believers their place of worship.[4]
- The colored people should not urge that they be placed on an equality with white people.[5]

Do these statements reflect the general wisdom of Ellen White, whom Adventists—both black and white—regard as the messenger of the Lord? How do we feel about these statements, and how do we relate to them?

One of the problems that lasted for decades is *that whites took these statements out of their historical context and created barriers between the races that lasted far longer than they were intended.* And blacks were hurt and confused by one they wanted to respect as the messenger of the Lord.

Ellen White's wisdom

What was Ellen White *really* saying? Let's look again at what she wrote in *Testimonies for the Church*, volume 9.

- Most decided efforts should be made to educate and train colored men and women to labor as missionaries in the Southern States of America. Christian colored students should be preparing to give the truth to their own race. Those who make the fear of the Lord the beginning of their wisdom and give heed to the counsel of men of experience can be a great blessing to the Negro race by carrying to their own people the light of present truth.[6]
- I am burdened, heavily burdened, for the work among the colored people. The gospel is to be presented to the down-

trodden Negro race. But great caution will have to be shown in the efforts put forth for the uplifting of this people. Among the white people in many places there exists a strong prejudice against the Negro race. We may desire to ignore this prejudice, but we cannot do it. If we were to act as if this prejudice did not exist we could not get the light before the white people. We must meet the situation as it is and deal with it wisely and intelligently.[7]

- Much might have been accomplished by the people of America if adequate efforts in behalf of the freedmen had been put forth by the Government and by the Christian churches immediately after the emancipation of the slaves.[8]

- Some of the strong Christian churches began a good work, but sadly failed to reach more than a comparatively few; and the Seventh-day Adventist Church has failed to act its part. . . .

  Noble efforts have been put forth by some Seventh-day Adventists to do the work that needed to be done for the colored people. Had those who were engaged in this work received the co-operation of all their ministering brethren, the result of their work would now be altogether different from what it is.[9]

- Let the colored believers be provided with neat, tasteful houses of worship. Let them be shown that this is done not to exclude them from worshiping with white people, because they are black, but in order that the progress of the truth may be advanced. Let them understand that this plan is to be followed *until the Lord shows us a better way.*[10]

- The colored ministers should make every effort possible to help their own people to understand the truth for this time. *As time advances, and race prejudices increase,* it will become almost impossible, in many places, for white workers to labor for the colored people. Sometimes the white people who are not in sympathy with our work will unite with colored people to oppose it, claiming that our teaching is an effort to break up churches and bring in trouble over the Sabbath question. White ministers and colored ministers will make false statements, arousing in the minds of the people such a feeling of antagonism that they will be ready to destroy and to kill.[11]

- Let us follow the course of wisdom. Let us do nothing that will unnecessarily arouse opposition—nothing that will hinder the proclamation of the gospel message. Where demanded by custom or where greater efficiency is to be gained, let the white believers and the colored believers assemble in separate places of worship.[12]

- When the Holy Spirit is poured out, there will be a triumph of humanity over prejudice in seeking the salvation of the souls of human beings. God will control minds. Human hearts will love as Christ loved. And the color line will be regarded by many very differently from the way in which it is now regarded.[13]

- We are to labor calmly, quietly, faithfully, trusting in our Elder Brother. We are not to be in haste to define the exact course to be pursued in the future regarding the relation to be maintained between white and colored people.[14]

- When the truth has been presented in a place, and as many white people as will hear and believe have accepted the truth, opportunities will sometimes appear for efforts to be made, in a quiet, unobtrusive manner, by white laborers for the colored people. Such opportunities should not be overlooked.

  But we must not unnecessarily arouse prejudice that would close the way against the proclamation of the third angel's message to the white people.[15]

- We must have faith in God—faith that He will arrange matters in a way that will enable us to work successfully. No one ever trusted God in vain. He will never disappoint those who put their trust in Him.

We are to avoid entering into contention over the problem of the color line. If this question is much agitated, difficulties will arise that will consume much precious time to adjust. We cannot lay down a definite line to be followed in dealing with this subject. In different places and under varying circumstances, the subject will need to be handled differently. In the South, where race prejudice is so strong, we could do nothing in presenting the truth were we to deal with the color line question as we can deal with it in some places in the North. The white workers in the South will have to move in a way that will enable them to gain access to the white people.[16]

- I know that if we attempt to meet the ideas and preferences of some of the colored people, we shall find our way blocked completely. The work of proclaiming the truth for this time is not to be hindered by an effort to adjust the position of the Negro race. Should we attempt to do this we should find that barriers like mountains would be raised to hinder the work that God desires to have done. If we move quietly and judiciously, laboring in the way that God has marked out, both white and colored people will be benefited by our labors.[17]

- *The time has not come* for us to work as if there were no prejudice. Christ said: "Be ye therefore wise as serpents, and harmless as doves." Matthew 10:16. If you see that by doing certain things which you have a perfect right to do, you hinder the advancement of God's work, refrain from doing those things. Do nothing that will close the minds of others against the truth. There is a world to save, and we shall gain nothing by cutting loose from those we are trying to help. All things may be lawful, but all things are not expedient.

The wise course is the best. As laborers together with God, we are to work in the way that will enable us to accomplish the most for Him. Let none go to extremes. We need wisdom from above; for we have a difficult problem to solve. *If rash moves are made now, great mischief will be done.* The matter is to be presented in such a way that the truly converted colored people will cling to the truth for Christ's sake, refusing to renounce one principle of sound Bible doctrine because they may think that the very best course is not being pursued toward the Negro race. . . .

We are to do as the Spirit of the Lord shall dictate, and agitate the subject of the color line as little as possible.[18]

Letters and manuscripts written during reconstruction

The following letters and manuscripts reveal Ellen White's mind and wisdom as God was helping her through the terrible time of the Reconstruction Period (1865–1925), generally speaking, a time when the South had to adjust to the end of slavery and its sociological and financial fallout.

- We have been eating of the large loaf, and have left the suffering, distressed people of the Southern regions starving for education, starving for spiritual advantages. By your actions you have said, "Am I my brother's keeper?". . . . The colored people might have been helped with much better prospects of success years ago than now. The work is now tenfold harder than it would have been then. But who will continue to dishonor God by their indolence, by their neglect, by passing by on the other side? Do not, I beseech you, look upon the hard field, groan a little, set two or three at work in one locality, a few in another, and provide them only enough for the bare necessaries of life. Those who labor in the Southern field will have to stand amid the most discouraging, hopeless poverty.[19]

- It is a shame for Christians who profess to be themselves redeemed by the blood of the Lamb to take a position to make these [colored] men feel that the mark of a humiliated race is upon them—*men standing in God's broad sunlight with mind and soul like other men, with as goodly a frame as has the best developed white man.* There are keenly sensitive minds that brood long and intensely over the oppressions suffered, and the slights they are made to feel. Many become jealous, soured, embittered, because of these prejudices, which make them feel every day that they are not like other men, not entitled even to worship God except in a prescribed manner. Even commiseration is humiliating, because it calls the sensitive mind to the misfortune that excites pity.[20]

- The Southern field has been presented to me as a difficult field to work, because of the white people who have the slave master's spirit with the slave master's cruelty in exercising the same, as if the blacks were no more than beasts; and to be treated worse than the dumb animals.[21]

- In one place the proposition was made that a curtain be drawn between the colored people and the white people. I asked, Would Jesus do that? This grieves the heart of Christ. The color of the skin is no criterion as to the value of the soul. By the mighty cleaver of truth we have all been quarried out from the world. God has taken us, all classes, all nations, all languages, all nationalities, and brought us into His workshop, to be prepared for His temple.[22]

What have we learned?

Ellen White does *not* say Adventists should have separate churches for blacks and whites *wherever possible.* She *did* say that, during the worst part of the Reconstruction period, in the 1890s and early 1900s, separate churches would be the wisest course "where demanded by custom or where greater efficiency is to be gained." With prophetic insight she saw a bigger picture—separate churches were not to be encouraged "because the believers are black" but because this was wise "until the Lord shows us a better way."

In God's eyes, Ellen White declares, there is no color line. But she saw the deepening troubles converging on the Southern black, and that "as time advances, and race prejudices increase, it will become almost impossible, in many places, for white workers to labor for the colored people." Thus for years, her counsel focused on the best way that the Adventist message could go to both blacks and whites under prevailing conditions. In other words, the encouragement she gave to both blacks and whites before the increase of Jim Crow laws and the prejudicial spirit became endemic had to be tempered by the reality of the changing scene, especially in the Southern states. When time, place, and circumstance is considered during these turbulent times, Ellen White did not contradict herself. Rather, she was a clarion voice whose moral clarity kept the Adventist Church from zigzagging too far in either direction.

Her moral *principles* regarding the color line, based on biblical foundations, are as valid today as when she was alive. But the *policies* she added to meet the changing circumstances of her day are no longer relevant or applicable today.

What was changing in the Southern states?

Ron Graybill has called the dark period between 1895–1910 "the betrayal of the Negro." He argued that "once the relevant aspects of Negro history during this period are grasped, what at first appears to be a contradiction in Ellen White's writings becomes understandable."[23]

Graybill chose these two dates arbitrarily, recognizing that in 1895, James Edson White, Ellen White's son, established his riverboat ministry in Vicksburg, Mississippi—also the same year in which Booker T. Washington made his famous Atlanta speech wherein he assumed virtually unrivaled leadership of Negro affairs in America. Graybill chose 1910 because it was close to 1908, the year in which Ellen White compiled her material in *Testimonies for the Church*, volume 9. However, "the long dark night" for Negroes extended into the 1920s and later.

Dark shadows began in the fateful "Compromise of 1877" by which Rutherford B. Hayes maneuvered his way into the White House, even after his opponent, Samuel J. Tilden, had won more than a quarter of a million more popular votes!

That Compromise, negotiated in the United States Congress, was a simple agreement to leave the South alone to work out its racial problems without interference from the federal government. Such a position is difficult to believe today, but such is the world of politics. The South soon forgot its pledges to the blacks. Although blacks had been given the right to vote, movements began to disenfranchise them.

Whatever one calls this period, it surely was the rule of white supremacy, white superiority, and black segregation. Keep in mind that President Woodrow Wilson *in 1913* ordered the segregating of federal office buildings in Washington, D.C.! And the nation's capital remained a segregated city well into the mid-twentieth century—a far cry from what President Lincoln had envisaged.

Ellen White saw clearly the plague of segregation

No wonder Ellen White wrote, "Much might have been accomplished by the people of America if adequate efforts in behalf of the freedmen had been put forth by the Government and by the Christian churches immediately after the emancipation of the slaves. Money should have been used freely to care for and educate them at the time they were so greatly in need of help. But the Government, after a little effort, left the Negro to struggle, unaided, with his burden of difficulties."[24]

Looking back, we can appreciate more clearly how the Lord led Ellen White through those murky years of mistrust, ignorance, and the eclipse of moral clarity. However, her confidence that circumstances would eventually change for the better was validated. Without Ellen White, the Adventist Church would have fractured along racial lines as quickly as did the Presbyterian, Methodist, and Baptist churches; and that gulf would have damaged the Advent movement, perhaps irretrievably, throughout the world field.

For many today, this black/white struggle seems as unreal as a Harry Potter movie. For others, the struggle appears to be under the church's radar. But for all of us, the social lessons that should be learned and practiced are as up-to-date as tomorrow's newspaper. And for many hundreds of thousands today—black and white—Ellen White's inspired wisdom remains the source of good judgment in resolving any lingering whispers of racial tension within the church.

---

1. Ellen G. White, *The Southern Work* (Washington, D.C.: Review and Herald® Publishing Association, 1966), 10–12.
2. E. G. White, *Testimonies for the Church*, 9:205 (see chap. 1, n. 5).
3. Ibid., 206.
4. Ibid., 210.
5. Ibid., 214.
6. Ibid., 199.
7. Ibid., 204.
8. Ibid., 205.
9. Ibid., 205.
10. Ibid., 206, 207, emphasis supplied.
11. Ibid., 207, 208, emphasis supplied.
12. Ibid., 208.
13. Ibid., 209.
14. Ibid., 209, 210.
15. Ibid., 210.

16. Ibid., 213.

17. Ibid., 214, 215.

18. Ibid., 215, emphasis supplied.

19. Ellen G. White, *Manuscript Releases*, vol. 4 (Silver Spring, Md.: E. G. White Estate, 1990), 2.

20. Ibid., 8.

21. Ibid., 11.

22. Ibid., 16, 17.

23. Ronald D. Graybill, *Ellen G. White and Church Race Relations* (Washington, D.C.: Review and Herald® Publishing Association, 1970), 17. This is a most helpful book.

24. E. G. White, *Testimonies for the Church*, 9:205.

Chapter Four

THE VISION THAT SAVED A CHURCH— CORE PRINCIPLES OF HEALTHFUL LIVING

No one saw it coming! No one before had ever set forth an integrated, interconnected health program that had stood the test of time!

Ellen White's Otsego, Michigan, health vision of June 6, 1863, lasted forty-five minutes, but its profound scope is continually validated by the latest medical research in the twenty-first century.

First, we will look at how this vision played out in the life of Ellen White herself. Next, we will review the general state of health enjoyed—if that is the right word!—by those in the middle 1880s. Then, we will take a fast cruise through the health principles presented in this vision—principles that soon became built into the fabric of the Adventist lifestyle. And we'll end with a brief overview of why these health principles have become more than a collection of great advice.

In 1844, when God called Ellen White to her prophetic ministry, she was a seventeen-year-old, frail, eighty-pound weakling who had to be carried by others. Physicians told her parents that she would die within months. She could speak only in whispers. But when the time came to reveal her visions, God gave her the strength to speak and to lean into the future with new courage. She outlived almost all her contemporaries and far exceeded them in terms of a productive life. She not only taught innovative and advanced principles of health, she lived them to the best of her ability, at times under the most difficult conditions. Her colleagues soon learned the advantages of following these principles, and most of them experienced dramatic changes in personal health. These principles have stood the test of more than a century, and contemporary research continues to validate her nineteenth-century teachings.

To better appreciate the distinctiveness of Ellen White's philosophy of health, let's review some of the health notions in vogue in her day. At the beginning of the nineteenth century, a remarkably standardized pattern for the treatment of disease relied "mostly on bleeding, purging, and polypharmacy [administering a mixture of drugs, most of them toxic]."[1]

The cause of disease was a matter of widely diverse conjecture. No one had a clear idea of invading organisms—germs—attacking specific parts of the body. The Christian world generally believed that illness and suffering were divinely inflicted because of sin. Healing, if possible, was the result of prayer and faith.

Whenever people occasionally raised the possibility that nature itself contained healing powers, as Hippocrates had believed centuries earlier, they were "confronted with the almost uniform opposition of the regular medical practitioners, who labeled them as empiric rustics attempting to restore a discredited element of primitive medicine."[2]

However, in 1860 Dr. Oliver Wendell Holmes, professor of anatomy at Harvard University, wrote that "if the whole materia medica, as now used, could be sunk to the bottom of the sea, it would be all the better for mankind—and all the worse for the fishes."[3]

In the second quarter of the nineteenth century, a remarkably fresh concern for personal health shifted the focus away from traditional theories and placed it on the individual.[4] Distrust of traditional medicine with its "heroic" treatments and pitiful results turned the minds of many in all classes to what could be done with common sense.[5] The result was a remarkable rise of new approaches to health and healing, such as the temperance movement;[6] vegetarianism;[7] public renunciation of "all evil habits" (tobacco, alcoholic beverages, tea, coffee, etc.);[8] development of "physiological" societies;[9] emphasis on public health, including sanitation and hospitals;[10] new attention to the health implications of fashion;[11] and the emergence of "water" treatments.[12]

But there was very little overlapping among these worthy movements. No integrating principle emerged to make all these movements more than passing fads—that is, not until June 6, 1863, and Ellen White's Otsego, Michigan, vision.

As the Sabbath was approaching, a small group of Adventists met in the Hilliard home and asked Ellen White to lead them in prayer. As she prayed, her voice changed, and they heard her exclaim, "Glory to God!" Martha Amadon, daughter of John Byington, the newly elected president of the General Conference, described the scene: "Those present at the time this vision was given will never forget the heavenly influence that filled the room. . . . Many who have witnessed these things have often wished a description could be given of the servant of God when thus under the influence of the Holy Spirit—the illumination of the countenance, the graceful gestures of the hands, the dignity attending every movement, the musical intonations of the voice sounding as from a distance, and many, many other things which give an eyewitness confidence in their heavenly origin."[13]

This vision dealt with many subjects of great interest, including definite instruction for Ellen's weary and overworked husband and a new challenge for Adventists to become teachers in the area of health in their homes and communities. But for Ellen and those listening, this vision opened before them "the great subject of health reform." In reviewing the vision, Ellen White said, "I was astonished at the things shown me in vision. Many things came directly across my own ideas. The matter was upon my mind continually. I talked it to all with whom I had opportunity to converse. My first writing of the vision was the substance of the matter contained in [Spiritual Gifts] Volume IV and in [my six articles in] *How to Live*, headed, 'Disease and Its Causes.' "[14]

In May 1866, she visited Dr. H. S. Lay, an Adventist physician in Allegan, Michigan. Fascinated with her vision summary, he wanted a full interview. Mrs. White responded reluctantly because she "was not familiar with medical language" and because "much of the matter presented to her was so different from the commonly accepted views that she feared she could not relate it so that it would be understood."[15]

Dr. Lay was impressed. Her insights were accurate, and the overall coherency of the message was profound. He knew that her description of the interacting nature of these principles did not come to her from human sources. He often related to others what he learned that day. Much later, he shared his discussion with Ellen White on health principles with one of his medical friends, Dr. John Harvey Kellogg. In 1897 Dr. Kellogg said, "It is a very interesting fact that the Lord began giving us this light thirty years ago. Just before I came to the Conference I had a talk with Dr. Lay, and he told me of how he heard the first instruction about health reform away back in 1860 and especially in 1863. While he was riding in a carriage with Brother and Sister White, she related what had been presented to her upon the subject of health reform, and laid out the principles which have stood the test of all these years—a whole generation."[16]

Speaking to the assembled delegates at the 1897 General Conference, Dr. Kellogg added:

> It is impossible for any man who has not made a special
> study of medicine to appreciate the wonderful character of the

instruction that has been received in these writings. It is wonderful, brethren, when you look back over the writings that were given us thirty years ago, and then perhaps the next day pick up a scientific journal and find some new discovery that the microscope has made, or that has been brought to light in the chemical laboratory—I say, it is perfectly wonderful how correctly they agree in fact. . . . There is not a single principle in relation to the healthful development of our bodies and minds that is advocated in these writings from Sister White, which I am not prepared to demonstrate conclusively from scientific evidence.[17]

While traveling on a brutal schedule, still mourning the sad death of Henry, her firstborn son, Ellen White rushed to completion *Spiritual Gifts*, volumes 3 and 4. Volume 4 included a section called "Health," which contained the first comprehensive statement on health principles since the Otsego vision.

Were Adventists ready for this next call for personal reform? So many orders for the book were received that an announcement was made in the *Review and Herald*, August 23, 1864: "The call for *Spiritual Gifts* is so great that we are unable to fill orders as soon as they are received. We have two binders at work, but today have not a single copy in the office."

Reports of immediate and beneficial results began to pour into the *Review and Herald*, the Adventist clearing house for information. Pastor Isaac Sanborn wrote that for ten years he had tried many remedies for his inflammatory rheumatism. Then, in the spring of 1864 he gave up pork, and a few months later he adopted a two-meal-a-day program without meat of any kind. He joyfully reported, "I enjoy as perfect health as probably can be enjoyed in this mortal state. I would not return to my old habits of eating for any consideration. . . . I thank God for the light He has given upon this subject."[18]

M. E. Cornell recounted how his wife lay at the point of death with typhoid: "We knew that to take the drugs of physicians would be in this case certain death." He applied hydrotherapy treatments, giving "nature a chance to throw off the disease." In a short while, as they united in prayer, Mrs. Cornell was out of danger.[19]

Ellen White was forthright about the changes that had come to her as she applied the counsel she passed on to others—counsel that, she wrote, "came directly across my own ideas." In her "Health" article, one year after the Otsego vision, she wrote:

> Since the Lord presented before me, in June, 1863, the subject of meat-eating in relation to health, I have left the use of meat. For a while it was rather difficult to bring my appetite to bread, for which, formerly, I have had but little relish. But by persevering, I have been able to do this. I have lived for nearly one year without meat. For about six months most of the bread upon our table has been unleavened cakes, made of unbolted wheat meal and water, and a very little salt. We use fruits and vegetables liberally. I have lived for eight months upon two meals a day.[20]

What was so electrifying, so sweeping, so full of promise in the Otsego health vision?[21] The core principles were as follows:

- Those who do not control their appetite in eating are guilty of intemperance.
- Swine's flesh was not to be eaten under any circumstance.
- Tobacco in any form is a slow poison.
- Strict cleanliness of the body and home premises is important.
- Tea and coffee, like tobacco, are slow poisons.
- Rich cake, pies, and puddings are injurious.
- Eating between meals injures the stomach and digestive process.

- Adequate time must be allowed between meals, giving the stomach time to rest.
- If a third meal is taken, it should be light and eaten several hours before bedtime.
- People used to meat, gravies, and pastries do not immediately relish a plain, wholesome diet.
- Gluttonous appetite contributes to indulgence of corrupt passions.
- Adopting a plain, nutritious diet may overcome the physical damage caused by a wrong diet.
- Reforms in eating will save expense and labor.
- Children eating flesh meat and spicy foods have strong tendencies toward sexual indulgences.
- Poisonous drugs used as medical prescriptions kill more people than all other causes of death combined.
- Pure water should be used freely in maintaining health and curing illnesses.
- Nature alone has curative powers.
- Common medicines, such as strychnine, opium, calomel, mercury, and quinine, are poisons.
- Parents transmit their weaknesses to their children; prenatal influences have enormous effects.
- Obeying the laws of health will prevent many illnesses.
- God is too often blamed for deaths caused by violation of nature's laws.
- Light and pure air, especially in the sleeping quarters, are required.
- On rising in the morning, bathing, even a sponge bath, will be beneficial. God will not work healing miracles for those who continually violate the laws of health.
- Many invalids have no physical cause for their illness; they have a diseased imagination.

- Physical labor, willingly performed, will help to create a healthy, cheerful disposition.
- Willpower has much to do with resisting disease and soothing nerves.
- Outdoor exercise is very important to health of mind and body. Overwork breaks down both mind and body; routine daily rest is necessary.
- Many die of disease caused wholly by eating flesh food.
- Caring for health is a spiritual matter, reflecting a person's commitment to God.
- A healthy mind and body directly affect one's morals and one's ability to discern truth.
- All God's promises are given on condition of obedience.

Clear, sensible, practical outline

These fundamental principles became the clear, sensible, practical outline of what has become known worldwide as the Seventh-day Adventist lifestyle.[22] Ellen White often amplified these core principles, most clearly in her 1905 volume *The Ministry of Healing*. One of her graphic statements that has galvanized millions is, "Pure air, sunlight, abstemiousness, rest, exercise, proper diet, the use of water, trust in divine power—these are the true remedies."[23]

For Adventists living in 1864, these health principles were indeed electrifying. Adventists had read and heard some of these principles before, but not within the spiritual context in which Ellen White placed them. Furthermore, Adventists now had a concise, coherent outline of health laws separated from the excesses and frivolities of others who were promoting lifestyle changes at the time.

Dr. Kellogg's endorsement

Dr. Kellogg put the question of "who told Ellen White about health reform?" into sharp perspective when he wrote the following passage in 1890 in his preface to the book *Christian Temperance and Bible Hygiene:*

Nearly thirty years ago there appeared in print the first of a series of remarkable and important articles on the subject of health, by Mrs. E. G. White. . . . Thousands were led to change life-long habits, and to renounce practices thoroughly fixed by heredity as well as by long indulgence. So great a revolution could not be wrought in a body of people, without the aid of some powerful incentive, which in this case was undoubtedly the belief that the writings referred to not only bore the stamp of truth, but were endorsed as such by a higher than human authority. . . .

At the time the writings referred to first appeared, the subject of health was almost wholly ignored, not only by the people to whom they were addressed, but by the world at large. The few advocating the necessity of a reform in physical habits, [also] propagated in connection with the advocacy of genuine reformatory principles the most patent and in some instances disgusting errors.

Nowhere, and by no one, was there presented a systematic and harmonious body of hygienic truths, free from patent errors, and consistent with the Bible and the principles of the Christian religion. . . .

Many of the principles taught have come to be so generally adopted and practiced that they are no longer recognized as reforms, and may, in fact, be regarded as prevalent customs among the more intelligent classes. The principles which a quarter of a century ago were either entirely ignored or made the butt of ridicule, have quietly won their way into public confidence and esteem, until the world has quite forgotten that they have not always been thus accepted. . . .

It certainly must be regarded as a thing remarkable, and evincing unmistakable evidence of divine insight and direction, that in the midst of confused and conflicting teachings claiming the authority of science and experience, but warped by ultra notions and rendered impotent for good by the great admixture of error—it must be admitted to be something extraordinary, that a person making no claims to scientific knowledge or erudition should have been able to organize, from the confused and error-tainted mass of ideas advanced by a few writers and thinkers on health subjects, a body of hygienic principles so harmonious, so consistent, and so genuine that the discussions, the researches, the discoveries, and the experience of a quarter of a century have not resulted in the overthrow of a single principle, but have only served to establish the doctrines taught.

The guidance of infinite wisdom is as much needed in the discerning between truth and error as in the evolution of new truths. Novelty is by no means a distinguishing characteristic of true principles, and the principle holds good as regards the truths of hygienic reform, as well as those of other reformatory movements.[24]

What should we make of Dr. Kellogg's unqualified endorsement of the impact of Ellen White's seminal health messages derived from her Otsego vision in 1863? In summary, these are Kellogg's conclusions:

- In 1863 health reform was "almost totally ignored" by Adventists and "the world at large."
- The few who were advocating "reform" included with their insights "the most patent and . . . disgusting errors."
- Before Ellen White's messages, no one had presented "a systematic and harmonious body of hygienic truths, free from

patent errors, and consistent with the Bible and the principles of the Christian religion."

- Thousands changed lifelong habits after reading these messages because they recognized not only the inherent harmony of these truths, but also their divine endorsement.
- Ellen White's principles have stood the test of time and experience.
- Many of those principles, ridiculed or ignored in 1863, had become accepted by 1890.
- Remarkable scientific discoveries since 1863 had only strongly fortified those principles, without "the overthrow of a single principle."
- Divine guidance is "as much needed" in distinguishing truth from error as "in the evolution of new truths."
- This record, spanning nearly thirty years, gives "unmistakable evidence of divine insight and direction" in the midst of "confused and conflicting teachings" in that a person "making no claims to scientific knowledge . . . should . . . organize, from the confused and error-tainted mass of ideas . . . , a body of hygienic principles so harmonious, so consistent, and so genuine."

But the underlying, integrating principle that Ellen White presented to the world was far more than how to live healthfully and longer. She consistently linked the health emphasis with the third angel's message, calling the relationship one that is as close as the "hand is with the body."[25] That is to say, the health message constituted a very important aspect of the "everlasting gospel" (Revelation 14:6).

This connection supplied the Adventist distinctive contribution to nineteenth-century health reform; the Adventist emphasis on health was to help "fit a people for the coming of the Lord." "If man will cherish the light God in mercy gives him upon health reform, he may be sanctified through the truth, and fitted for immortality."[26]

Ellen White was specific and practical as she joined the spiritual with the physical and the mental. Placing health matters within the context of the three angels' messages of Revelation 14 raised the health issue from personal opinion to the level of spiritual commitment and character development. Health principles were linked with spiritual goals:

Our first duty to God and man is self-development. The following creative statement by Mrs. White has inspired many young people: "Our first duty toward God and our fellow beings is that of self-development. . . . Hence that time is spent to good account which is used in the establishment and preservation of physical and mental health. We cannot afford to dwarf or cripple any function of body or mind."[27]

Heart reform comes before health reform. Ellen White kept her priorities straight—preserving health is primarily a spiritual challenge: "Men will never be truly temperate until the grace of Christ is an abiding principle in the heart. . . . No mere restriction of your diet will cure your diseased appetite. . . . What Christ works within, will be worked out under the dictation of a converted intellect. The plan of beginning outside and trying to work inward has always failed, and always will fail."[28]

Health reform is part of the preparation for the latter rain and the loud cry. This application of health principles is profound and distinctively an Adventist insight. Ellen White wrote in 1867,

> God's people are not prepared for the loud cry of the third angel. They have a work to do for themselves which they should not leave for God to do for them. . . . Lustful appetite makes slaves of men and women, and beclouds their intellects and stupefies their moral sensibilities to such a degree that the sa-

cred, elevated truths of God's Word are not appreciated. . . . In order to be fitted for translation, the people of God must know themselves. . . . They should ever have the appetite in subjection to the moral and intellectual organs.[29]

Health is closely linked with sanctification. Ellen White was not hesitant in pointing to the direct relationship between daily habits and character development. She wrote, "A diseased body and disordered intellect, because of continual indulgence in hurtful lust, make sanctification of the body and spirit impossible."[30] For "those who have received instruction regarding the evils of the use of flesh foods, tea, and coffee, and rich and unhealthful food preparations, . . . God demands that the appetite be cleansed, and that self-denial be practiced. . . . This is a work that will have to be done before His people can stand before Him a perfected people."[31]

Adventist leaders such as J. H. Waggoner saw the distinctive difference between contemporary voices appealing for health reform and the advanced principles Ellen White espoused. Waggoner wrote,

We do not profess to be pioneers in the general principles of the health reform. The facts on which this movement is based have been elaborated, in a great measure, by reformers, physicians, and writers on physiology and hygiene, and so may be found scattered through the land. But we do claim that by the method of God's choice it has been more clearly and powerfully unfolded, and is thereby producing an effect which we could not have looked for from any other means.

As mere physiological and hygienic truths, they might be studied by some at their leisure, and by others laid aside as of little consequence; but when placed on a level with the great truths of the third angel's message by the sanction and authority of God's Spirit, and so declared to be the means whereby a

weak people may be made strong to overcome, and our diseased bodies cleansed and fitted for translation, then it comes
to us as an essential part of present truth, to be received with
the blessing of God, or rejected at our peril.[32]

*A commitment to health is among the factors relating to a prepared
people.* Ellen White directly linked a person's commitment to physical
and spiritual health with his or her readiness for eternal life. Here again
"restoration"[33]—the goal of the great controversy theme—determined the philosophy of health.

Regarding the kind of people prepared for Jesus' return, Mrs. White
wrote, "We believe without a doubt that Christ is soon coming. . . .
When He comes He is not to cleanse us of our sins, to remove from us
the defects in our characters, or to cure us of the infirmities of our
tempers and dispositions. If wrought for us at all, this work will all be
accomplished before that time. When the Lord comes, those who are
holy will be holy still. Those who have preserved their bodies and spirits in holiness, in sanctification and honor, will then receive the finish-
ing touch of immortality."[34]

Ellen White boldly encouraged church members who sensed "the
dead level into which they have fallen" to reconnect the health message to the theological message: "Send into the churches workers
who will set the principles of health reform in their connection with
the third angel's message before every family and individual. Encour-
age all to take a part in work for their fellowmen, and see if the breath
of life will not quickly return to these churches."[35]

The great controversy theme seeks "restoration" as the goal of salvation. Whatever subject Ellen White focuses on, this goal integrates
all of its aspects. Thus the great controversy theme informs the basis
and purpose of health reform. It naturally follows, then, that the physician and the minister are to "work in tandem. Like harnessed horses,
they . . . [are] to pull the Adventist carriage at the same speed."[36]

In the developing years of Adventist health work, Ellen White riveted her contemporaries on the importance of joining health reform with the completion of the gospel commission. For her, the gospel evangelist/minister and the gospel healer were to work together with mutual aims and joint evangelistic efforts.[37]

The record stands: Compared to the relatively few "health reformers" in her day, Ellen White was unique. When compared to or contrasted with conventional medical wisdom and practice, she was decades ahead of her time. And no one had ever connected the health of the body and mind with spiritual preparation for moral stamina in this life and thus for fitness to live forever.

In what other ways was Ellen White unique in her insights on health? Contemporary health reformers were prescient in some areas, but gravely wrong in others. Many held extreme positions on "discarding milk, sugar, and salt," etc.[38] Others believed that rest, not physical exercise, was indicated for those recuperating from illness. What if Ellen White had held these and other extreme positions? Her credibility would have been severely damaged in the ensuing years. More than that, if she had endorsed contemporary medical knowledge, her credibility would have been demolished.

But the health principles found in her nineteenth-century writings, distinctively coherent, have stood the test of time. Her principles relating to prevention of disease as well as the restoration of health are not viewed as fads today.

The vision of 1863 and others that followed to fill out the information of the Otsego vision will be studied until Jesus returns by those who would rather say Yes to God's counsel and not No.[39]

---

1. George W. Reid, *A Sound of Trumpets* (Washington, D.C.: Review and Herald® Publishing Association, 1982), 16.

2. Ibid., 28.

3. Ronald L. Numbers, *Prophetess of Health* (New York: Harper & Row, 1976), 49.

4. Malcolm Bull and Keith Lockhart, *Seeking a Sanctuary* (San Francisco: Harper & Row, 1989), 128.

5. Rennie B. Schoepflin, "Health and Health Care," *The World of Ellen G. White*, ed. Gary Land (Washington, D.C.: Review and Herald® Publishing Association, 1987), 143–158.

6. Jerome L. Clark, "The Crusade Against Alcohol," in Land, *The World of Ellen G. White*, 131–140; Stephen Nissenbaum, *Sex, Diet, and Debility in Jacksonian America* (Chicago: The Dorsey Press, 1980), 69–85; D. E. Robinson, *The Story of Our Health Message* (Nashville, Tenn.: Southern Publishing Association, 1965), 38–42.

7. Nissenbaum, *Sex, Diet, and Debility*, 39–52; Reid, *A Sound of Trumpets*, 85; Robinson, *Our Health Message*, 42–47.

8. Reid, *A Sound of Trumpets*, 42, 43.

9. Ibid., p. 37; Robinson, *Our Health Message*, 47, 48.

10. Schoepflin, in Land, *The World of Ellen G. White*, 151–157.

11. Ibid., 155.

12. Ibid., 146–148; Reid, *A Sound of Trumpets*, 79–81; Robinson, *Our Health Message*, 28–37. See also Numbers, *Prophetess of Health*, 48–76.

13. Arthur L. White, *Ellen G. White: The Progressive Years*, 1862–1876 (Washington, D.C.: Review and Herald® Publishing Association, 1986), 17.

14. Ellen G. White, *Selected Messages*, vol. 3 (Washington, D.C.: Review and Herald® Publishing Association, 1980), 281.

15. Robinson, *Our Health Message*, 83.

16. *General Conference Daily Bulletin,* March 8, 1897, 309, cited in Robinson, *Our Health Message*, 83, 84.

17. Ibid., 84.

18. *Review and Herald*, April 11, 1865.

19. Robinson, *Our Health Message*, 96.

20. Ellen G. White, *Spiritual Gifts*, vol. 4 (Washington, D.C.: Review and Herald, 1945) 153, cited in Robinson, *Our Health Message*, 94. For a continuing record of Ellen White's experience with health reform principles, plus her principles of common sense, see Ellen G. White, *Testimonies for the Church*, 2:362–390.

21. E. G. White, *Spiritual Gifts*, vol. 4, 120–151. See Ellen G. White, *Counsels on Diet and Foods* (Washington, D.C.: Review and Herald® Publishing Association, 1946), 481–494.

22. *Time*, October 28, 1966, referred to the astounding statistical differences in health and mortality between California Adventist men and the general population as "The Adventist Advantage."

23. Ellen G. White, *The Ministry of Healing* (Mountain View, Calif.: Pacific Press® Publishing Association, 1942),127. See also E. G. White, *Testimonies for the Church*, 5:443 (see chap. 1, n. 5).

24. *Christian Temperance and Bible Hygiene* (Battle Creek: Good Health Publi-

cation Company, 1890). The preface does not name its author as Dr. J. H. Kellogg. However, in his presentation to the General Conference session on March 3, 1897, Dr. Kellogg said, "Now in the preface to *Christian Temperance* you will find a statement which I presume not very many of you have read. There is no name signed to the preface, but I wrote it. But if you will read it, you will find a statement to the effect that every single statement with reference to healthful living, and the general principles that underlie the subject, have been verified by scientific discovery. I sometimes see some of our brethren appear to be a little shaky on the testimonies; they do not know whether these things come from the Lord or not; but to those I invariably say that if you will study the subject of health reform from the testimonies, and then from the light of scientific discovery—compare it with what science teaches at the present time—you will be amazed; you will see what a flood of light was given us thirty years ago. There is, however, a more amazing thing than that, and it is that this light which was given to us at that time, confirmed as it is by scientific discovery—I say the most amazing thing of all is that we as a people have turned our backs upon this, and have not accepted it, and believed in it as we should. I want to repeat it that there is not a single principle in relation to the healthful development of our bodies and minds that is advocated in these writings from Sister White, which I am not prepared to demonstrate conclusively from scientific evidence." Ellen White wrote that part of the book called *Christian Temperance*, and the portion called *Bible Hygiene* was written by her husband, James White.

25. E. G. White, *Testimonies for the Church*, 3:62.

26. Ibid., 161; *The Health Reformer*, October 1, 1872.

27. E. G. White, *Counsels on Diet and Foods*, 15; see also Ellen G. White, *Christ's Object Lessons* (Washington, D.C.: Review and Herald® Publishing Association, 1941), 329.

28. Ibid., 35.

29. Ibid., 32, 33.

30. Ibid., 44.

31. Ibid., 381.

32. *Review and Herald*, August 7, 1866.

33. See Ellen G. White, *The Desire of Ages* (Mountain View, Calif.: Pacific Press® Publishing Association, 1940), 824; Ellen G. White, *Education* (Mountain View, Calif.: Pacific Press® Publishing Association, 1952), 125.

34. E. G. White, *Testimonies for the Church*, 2:355.

35. Ellen G. White, *Testimonies to Ministers and Gospel Workers* (Mountain View, Calif.: Pacific Press® Publishing Association, 1962), 416. "Make regular, organized efforts to lift the church members out of the dead level in which they have been for years. Send out into the churches workers who will live the principles of health reform. Let those be sent who can see the necessity of self-denial in appetite, or they will be a snare to the church. See if the breath of life will not then come into

our churches. A new element needs to be brought into the work."—E. G. White, *Testimonies for the Church*, 6:267.

36. Bull and Lockhart, *Seeking a Sanctuary*, 219.

37. "I wish to speak about the relation existing between the medical missionary work and the gospel ministry. It has been presented to me that every department of the work is to be united in one great whole. The work of God is to prepare a people to stand before the Son of man at His coming, and this work should be a unit. The work that is to fit a people to stand firm in the last great day must not be a divided work. . . .

"Gospel workers are to minister on the right hand and on the left, doing their work intelligently and solidly. There is to be no division between the ministry and the medical work. The physician should labor equally with the minister, and with as much earnestness and thoroughness for the salvation of the soul, as well as for the restoration of the body."—*Medical Ministry*, 237. "The Holy Spirit never has, and never will in the future, divorce the medical missionary work from the gospel ministry. They cannot be divorced. Bound up with Jesus Christ, the ministry of the word and the healing of the sick are one."—Manuscript 21, 1906, cited in Ellen G. White, *Special Testimonies,* series B, no. 7.

38. E. G. White, *Testimonies for the Church,* 3:19.

39. Key sources for further study: A. L. White, *The Early Years,* 6–22 (see chap. 1, n. 4); Douglass, *Messenger of the Lord,* 278–337 (see chap. 2, n. 1).

Chapter Five

THE RISE OF THE PAPACY—EVERYBODY'S HOLY FATHER

The virtual imprisonment of Pope Pius VI in 1798 by the French general Berthier signaled the death knell of the papacy—the religio-political power that had ruled Europe for more than a thousand years. Or so everyone thought!

The authority of the papacy had been diminishing for some time, especially following two events in the last half of the eighteenth century— a humiliating rebuff of the pope in 1782 by Emperor Joseph II in Vienna, and the worldwide suppression of the Jesuits by Pope Clement XIV in 1773. One historian described the papacy at the end of the eighteenth century as "very near its nadir." During the following decades, nobody in the Vatican, or anywhere else, foresaw the recovery of the papacy as a world power—except Ellen White! One can imagine how keen observers might scratch their heads in disbelief when, in 1884, they read

A day of great intellectual darkness has been shown to be favorable to the success of popery. It will yet be demonstrated that a day of great intellectual light is equally favorable for its success. . . .

In the movements now in progress in this country [the United States] to secure for the institutions and usages of the church the support of the State, Protestants are following in the steps of papists. Nay, more, they are opening the door for popery to regain in Protestant America the supremacy which she has lost in the Old World. And that which gives greater significance to this movement is the fact that the principal object contemplated is the enforcement of Sunday observance—a custom which originated with Rome, and which she claims as the sign of her authority.[1]

A few months later she wrote,

By the decree enforcing the institution of the papacy in violation of the law of God, our nation will disconnect herself fully from righteousness. When Protestantism shall stretch her hand across the gulf to grasp the hand of the Roman power, when she shall reach over the abyss to clasp hands with spiritualism, when, under the influence of this threefold union, our country shall repudiate every principle of its Constitution as a Protestant and republican government, and shall make provision for the propagation of papal falsehoods and delusions, then we may know that the time has come for the marvelous working of Satan and that the end is near.[2]

Then in 1886, Ellen White pressed this forecast further:

How the Roman Church can clear herself from the charge of idolatry we cannot see. . . . And this is the religion which Protestants are beginning to look upon with so much favor, and which will eventually be united with Protestantism. This union will not, however, be effected by a change in Catholicism; for Rome never changes. She claims infallibility. It is Protestantism that will change. The adoption of liberal ideas on its part will bring it where it can clasp the hand of Catholicism.[3]

An analysis of Ellen White's predictions

Let's analyze what Mrs. White predicted in the 1880s regarding these issues:

- Sunday sacredness would be established by law in the United States.
- Protestants would be foremost to "grasp the hand of the Roman power."
- This union would lead the United States to "repudiate every principle of its Constitution as a Protestant and republican government."
- This incredible union would occur, not because the papacy would concede anything, but because Protestantism would change due to its "adoption of liberal ideas."
- The passage of this Sunday "law" would signal "that the end is near."

Perhaps Ellen White's most complete prediction of papal influence in the end time is found in two chapters in *The Great Controversy* (written in 1888 and revised in 1911)—"Liberty of Conscience Threatened" and "The Impending Conflict." In these two chapters Mrs. White extended further some of the insights noted above:

> Protestants little know what they are doing when they propose to accept the aid of Rome in the work of Sunday exaltation. While they are bent upon the accomplishment of their purpose, Rome is aiming to re-establish her power, to recover her lost supremacy. Let the principle once be established in the United States that the church may employ or control the power of the state; that religious observances may be enforced by secular laws; in short, that the authority of church and state is to

dominate the conscience, and the triumph of Rome in this country is assured.

God's word has given warning of the impending danger; let this be unheeded, and the Protestant world will learn what the purposes of Rome really are, only when it is too late to escape the snare. She is silently growing into power.[4]

Additional insights

Here we are given additional insights into the implications of the future growth of the papacy not seen by others in 1888:

- Protestants do not realize what is at stake when they collaborate with the papacy in honoring Sunday sacredness.
- When the United States determines that it is constitutionally acceptable to enforce religious observances by legislation, precedence will be given for the enactment of Sunday laws.
- In the late nineteenth century, the papacy was "silently growing into power."

Those reading her words when they were first written might be pardoned for thinking that they reflected pure fantasy, given the current circumstances. However, for us living today, have we seen any developments on the world stage in the last twenty-five years that would suggest she knew what she was talking about? To say that we have is an understatement! Later in this chapter we will review some of the high points of recent decades that corroborate her predictions regarding the prominence the papacy would come to enjoy in the religious world in the end time.

Some reasons Protestants will grow closer to Catholics

Ellen White went on to list a number of reasons for the increased admiration and high regard Protestants and secular world leaders would come to have for the papacy in the end time:

- "An increasing indifference concerning the doctrines that separate the reformed churches from the papal hierarchy."[5]
- "Defenders of the papacy declare that the church has been maligned, and the Protestant world are inclined to accept the statement."[6]
- "Protestants have tampered with and patronized [Catholicism]; they have made compromises and concessions which [Catholics] themselves are surprised to see and fail to understand."[7]
- "The religious service of the Roman Church is a most impressive ceremonial. Its gorgeous display and solemn rites fascinate the senses of the people and silence the voice of reason and of conscience."[8]
- "The church's claim to the right to pardon leads [Catholics] to feel at liberty to sin; and the ordinance of confession, without which her pardon is not granted, tends also to give license to evil."[9]
- "The Roman Church now presents a fair front to the world, covering with apologies her record of horrible cruelties."[10]
- "As the Protestant churches have been seeking the favor of the world, false charity has blinded their eyes. They do not see but that it is right to believe good of all evil; and as the inevitable result, they will finally believe evil of all good."[11]
- "The Papacy is well adapted to meet the wants of all these. It is prepared for two classes of mankind, embracing nearly the whole world—those who would be saved by their merits, and those who would be saved in their sins. Here is the secret of its power."[12]

Protestants will open the door

In view of these eight characteristics of the Catholic Church that Ellen White predicted for the end time, what developments should we be expecting, ever keeping in mind Revelation 13–18?[13]

First, strange as it may seem, Protestants in the United States will open the door for the Catholic Church, making it possible for the Catholic Church to regain "in Protestant America the supremacy which she has lost in the Old World."[14] How can this be? "Through the timeserving concessions of the so-called Protestant world."[15]

Second, in some remarkable manner, the scenes of the past that "clearly reveal the enmity of Rome toward the true Sabbath and its defenders . . . are to be repeated as Roman Catholics and Protestants shall unite for the exaltation of the Sunday."[16] In fact, "in both the Old and the New World, the papacy will receive homage in the honor paid to the Sunday institution, that rests solely upon the authority of the Roman Church."[17]

Third, in a prediction that carries with it ominous conflicts of interest, she declares that

> the Roman Catholic Church, with all its ramifications throughout the world, forms one vast organization under the control, and designed to serve the interests, of the papal see. Its millions of communicants . . . are instructed to hold themselves as bound in allegiance to the pope. Whatever their nationality or their government, they are to regard the authority of the church as above all other. Though they may take the oath pledging their loyalty to the state, yet back of this lies the vow of obedience to Rome, absolving them from every pledge inimical to her interests.[18]

Consider the plight of the Roman Catholic legislator or judge in matters of religious concern. *Who has his or her higher allegiance—a nation's constitution or the church's dogma?*

Fourth, with this conflict of interest in place, it is not difficult to imagine how, even in the United States, "the church may employ or control the power of the state; that religious observances may be enforced by secular laws; in short, that the authority of church and state is to dominate the conscience, and the triumph of Rome in this country is assured."[19] Even now, by noting the rising number of Catholic legislators and judges in the United States, we can see that "she [the Roman Catholic Church] is silently growing into power. Her doctrines are exerting their influence in legislative halls, in the churches, and in the hearts of men."[20]

Pope John Paul II since 1976

Let's pause for a moment and look back over some of the major events in the religious world over the last few decades, particularly in the Roman Catholic Church and the career of Pope John Paul II. What has been the astonishing record since 1976?

September 1976. An obscure Polish archbishop from Krakow stood before an audience in New York City and made "one of the most prophetic speeches ever given: 'We are standing in the face of the greatest historical confrontation humanity has gone through . . . a test of two thousands years of culture and Christian civilization, and with all of its consequences for human dignity, individual rights and the rights of nations. . . . wide circles of American society and wide circles of the Christian community do not realize this fully.' " In only two years, that Polish archbishop would become Pope John Paul II.[21]

September 28, 1978. After being Pope for thirty-three days, Albino Luciani, now known as Pope John Paul, died. During this short time, he had initiated several courses of action that would have changed the direction of one-fifth of the world's population, especially in such areas as the role of Masonry among Catholics, artificial forms of birth control, and irregularities at the Vatican bank. It seemed he was a targeted man.[22]

October 16, 1978. The College of Cardinals at the Vatican elected Polish Cardinal Karol Wojtyla as pope. Wojtyla took the name John Paul II.

October 30, 1978. Pope John Paul II said, "We are now facing the final confrontation between the church and the antichurch, of the Gospel vs. the anti-Gospel."[23]

May 13, 1981. Two and a half years into his pontificate, Pope John Paul II was shot by a professional "hit man" in St. Peter's Square in the presence of some seventy-eight thousand people and before eleven million watching on television. Not an isolated moment, it was "entirely predictable, indeed inevitable" in the wake of his "fast-growing geopolitical presence."[24] Already, John Paul could not be ignored.

June 7, 1982. President Ronald Reagan and Pope John Paul II talked for fifty minutes in the Vatican Library, a conversation later called "one of the great secret alliances of all time"; its purpose—the collapse of the Soviet Union and the encouragement of reform movements in Hungary, Czechoslovakia, and the Pope's beloved Poland.[25]

September 22, 1983. Dan Quayle appealed to the United States Senate, "Under the courageous leadership of Pope John Paul II, the Vatican State has assumed its rightful place in the world as an international voice. It is only right that this country show its respect for the Vatican by diplomatically recognizing it as a world state."[26] In the following year, President Reagan appointed the first ambassador to the Vatican (not a personal representative), thereby recognizing for the first time the political significance of the central government of the Roman Catholic Church.[27]

December 1, 1989. At a Vatican summit, President Gorbachev and Pope John Paul II represented two contrasting visions of a "new world order." When Gorbachev addressed the Pope as "the world's highest moral authority," he recognized that he was not dealing with a "straw man."[28] Several years later, Gorbachev said, "I have carried on an intensive correspondence with Pope John Paul II since we met at the Vatican in December 1989. And I think ours will be an ongoing dialogue. . . . I am certain that the actions undertaken by John Paul II will play an enormous political role now that profound changes have occurred in European history."[29]

1989. The collapse of the Soviet Union was due in large part to the "great secret alliance"; and "the rush to freedom in Eastern Europe is a sweet victory for John Paul II."[30] "While Gorbachev's hands-off policies were the immediate cause of the chain reaction of liberty that has swept over Eastern Europe in the past few months, John Paul deserves much of the longer-range credit."[31]

1990. Malachi Martin's *The Keys of This Blood* [32] was published. This has to be considered one of the most astounding events of the century dealing with the aspirations and strategies of a pope. His phenomenal focus on Pope John Paul II staggers the mind as he outlines the Pope's strategy for world domination that (at the time of this printing) is being worked out with astounding rapidity.

May 1, 1991. Pope John Paul II released *"Centesimus Annus"* "(The Hundredth Year: On the Hundredth Anniversary of *Rerum Novarum*)," a remarkable *restatement* of Pope Leo XIII's overview of the rights of workers worldwide and how various government forms deny these rights. Ironically, both popes argued for religious liberty for all and yet called for government recognition of Sunday as the workers' day of rest and worship.[33]

February 24, 1992. Time magazine's cover story was titled "The Holy Alliance—How Reagan and the Pope Conspired to Assist Poland's Solidarity Movement and Hasten the Demise of Communism: An Investigative Report." Carl Bernstein reported, "Step by reluctant step, the Soviets and the communist government of Poland bowed to the moral, economic, and political presence imposed by the Pope and the President."[34]

Summer 1993, Colorado World Youth Day. After the Pope's visit to Colorado, the Vatican sensed a new opportunity to forge with the United States a plan to exert a "moral authority in world affairs."[35]

January 1994. Israel and the Vatican signed a "fundamental agreement" after forty-five years of troubled relationships. Israeli diplomats say that "the agreement acknowledges the inherent stake of the

Catholic Church in the Holy Land; the church is not a guest . . . but part and parcel of the reality of Israel."[36]

March 29, 1994. "Evangelicals and Catholics Together: The Christian Mission in the 3rd Millennium" was issued—a meeting and document that many say reversed five hundred years of church history. To imply that both sides preach the same Christ, understand authority and the "church" the same way, or hold the same understanding of "justification by grace through faith" is a test of credulity, but both sides "contend together" to uphold "sanctity of life, family values, parental choice in education, moral standards in society, and democratic institutions worldwide." The document further stated, "We affirm that a common set of core values is found in the teachings of religions, and that these form the basis of a global ethic . . . and which are the conditions for a sustainable world order." New phrases such as the church being responsible "for the right ordering of civil society" are more than interesting. Further, Evangelicals and Catholics agree that "it is neither theologically legitimate nor a prudent use of resources" to proselytize among active members of another Christian community.[37] Many rightfully called this "an historic moment."[38]

September 5–13, 1994. The International Conference on Population and Development in Cairo demonstrated to the world the political clout of Pope John Paul II. Surprisingly, the papacy joined with Muslim leaders in protesting proabortion phrases and funding that included abortion as a method for family planning. This coalition and its combined clout awakened the world to many liaisons through the decade in which Muslims and Catholics have been working together on common concerns.

October 16, 1994. Israel's first ambassador to the Vatican said his meeting with the Pope opened a "new epoch of cooperation." The Pope expressed his long-standing request for "international guarantees" to protect the "sacred character of Jerusalem," a city sacred to Christians, Muslims, and Jews.[39]

November 10, 1994. In his apostolic letter *"Tertio Millennio Adveni-ente"* ("The Coming Third Millennium"), the Pope built on the new era inaugurated by Vatican II—the "profound renewal" that opened up the Catholic Church to other Christians, the focus of each year from 1995 to the Grand Jubilee year of 2000, symbolic journeys to Bethle-hem, Jerusalem, and Mount Sinai "as a means of furthering dialogue with Jews and the followers of Islam, and to arranging similar meet-ings elsewhere with the leaders of the great world religions." The time between 1994 and 2000 were busy indeed as the Pope fulfilled the plans laid out in this letter.[40]

November 13, 1994. In harmony with a conservative Christian agenda that has been developing for decades, Charles Colson wrote in his col-umn "Why Catholics Are Our Allies," "Believers on the front lines, bat-tling issues such as abortion, pornography, and threats to religious liberty, find themselves sharing foxholes with conservatives across denominational lines—forging what theologian Timothy George calls 'an ecumenism of the trenches'. . . . The great divides within Christen-dom no longer fall along denominational lines but between conser-vatives and liberals *within* denominations. . . . Let's be certain that we are firing our polemical rifles against the enemy, not against those fighting in the trenches alongside us in defense of the Truth."[41]

December 26, 1994. Time magazine named John Paul II "Man of the Year." The accompanying article stated, "People who see him—and countless millions have—do not forget him. His appearances gener-ate electricity unmatched by anyone else on earth. . . . When he talks, it is not only to his flock of nearly a billion; he expects the world to listen. . . . In a year when so many people lamented the decline in moral values or made excuses for bad behavior, Pope John Paul II forcefully set forth his vision of the good life and urged the world to follow it. . . . John Paul's impact on the world has already been enormous, ranging from the global to the personal. . . . With increased urgency . . . John Paul presented himself, the defender of Roman Catholic doctrine, as a moral compass for believers and nonbelievers alike. . . . Billy Graham said, 'He's been the strong conscience of the whole Christian world.' "[42]

January 21, 1995. In Colombo, Sri Lanka, "Pope John Paul II ended an exhausting Asian tour with a call for the world's great religions to unite on behalf of shared moral values."[43]

May 25, 1995. The papal encyclical *"Ut Unum Sint"* ("That They May Be One") laid out, unambiguously, a powerful strategy for church unity, on one front to develop a nonconfrontational relationship with Islam, on the other, throughout the Christian world. This document committed the Roman Catholic Church to full communion with the Eastern Orthodox Church, a unity more important than jurisdiction. And he reminded the Protestant churches that the "Petrine ministry" belongs to all Christians, whether they recognize it or not.[44]

October 7, 1995. When Pope John Paul II presided at a mass in New York's Central Park, an estimated 125,000 people turned out to see, not only the leader of the world's largest Christian church, but also an ecumenical procession of Protestant, Orthodox, and other non-Catholic religious leaders, including "political power broker Pat Robertson at the head of the line." After the mass and an intimate visit with the Pope, Robertson "insisted that a new day is dawning in the relationship between conservative Protestants and traditional Roman Catholics."[45]

July 7, 1998. "*Dies Domini*" ("The Lord's Day"). From the first sentence, the Pope focused on "the Lord's Day—as Sunday was called from Apostolic times." The entire document is an amazing exercise in subtle misinterpretation of the biblical evidence, but very persuasive to the surface reader. Of the eighty-seven sections in the document, note the following: "62: It is the duty of Christians therefore to remember that, although the practices of the Jewish Sabbath are gone, surpassed as they are by the 'fulfillment' which Sunday brings, the underlying reasons for keeping 'the Lord's Day' holy—inscribed solemnly in the Ten Commandments—remain valid, though they need to be reinterpreted in the light of the theology and spirituality of Sunday.... 66: ... My predecessor Pope Leo XIII in his Encyclical *Rerum Novarum* spoke of Sunday rest as a worker's right which the State must guarantee.... 67: ... Therefore, also in the particular circumstances of our own time, Christians will naturally strive to ensure that civil legislations respects their duty to keep Sunday holy."[46]

October 27, 28, 1998. Archbishop Jean-Louis Tauran said that Jerusalem "has long been at the centre of the Holy See's concerns and one of its top priorities for international action.... The Holy See believes in the importance of extending representation at the negotiating table: in order to be sure that no aspect of the problem is overlooked."[47]

October 30, 1998. A nine-page document signed by Cardinal Ratzinger (who would become Pope Benedict XVI on April 19, 2005) emphasized that popes alone can determine the limits of those negotiating for the Vatican. Publicly, Ratzinger said that "it is clear that only the pope ... as successor of Peter, has the authority and the competence to speak the last word on the means of exercising the pastoral ministry of the universal truth." "The papacy," he said, "is not an office of the presidency ... and cannot be conceived of as a type of political monarchy."[48]

May 12, 1999. The Anglican-Roman Catholic International Commission (consisting of eighteen members), continuing a dialogue that began in 1981, published a statement containing some amazing areas of agreement, such as: "62. An experience of universal primacy of this kind would confirm two particular conclusions we have reached: (1) that Anglicans be open to and desire a recovery and re-reception under certain clear conditions of the exercise of universal primacy by the Bishop or Rome; and (2) that Roman Catholics be open to and desire a re-reception of the exercise of primacy by the Bishop of Rome and the offering of such a ministry to the whole Church of God."[49]

September 1, 1999; March 8, 12, 23, 2000. The Pope apologized for "past mistakes, . . . and to ask pardon for . . . historical offenses. . . . The wounds of the past, for which both sides share the guilt, continue to be a scandal for the world." Auxiliary Archbishop Rino Fisichella of Rome said of the March 12 meeting in St. Peter's: "Pope John Paul II wanted to give a complete global vision, making references to circumstances of the past, but without focusing on details out of respect for history. . . .The Church is not the one who has sinned, the sinners are Christians, and they have done so against the Church, the bride of Christ."[50]

October 31, 1999. In the same Reformation Church in which the Confession of the Princes was presented to Charles V in 1530, and 482 years to the day after Martin Luther nailed his ninety-five theses to the door of the village church in Wittenberg, the Lutheran World Federation (which does not include all branches of the Lutheran Church, such as the Missouri Synod) signed with Roman Catholics a "Joint Declaration on the Doctrine of Justification," after thirty years of consultation.

Four hundred years ago, Protestants and Catholics were in profound disagreement over the doctrine of justification, leading to vicious, deadly consequences. The "Joint Declaration on the Doctrine of Justification" is just one more example of how diminished the clarity of truth is today and how much "relationship" and "unity" have emerged as the most important issues for so many leading voices in modern Christianity.[51]

November 7, 1999. In New Delhi, India, Pope John Paul II, recognizing Catholicism's minority status in India, said that "no state, no group has the right to control either directly or indirectly a person's religious convictions . . . or the respectful appeal of a particular religion to people's free conscience."[52]

July 27, 2000. The United States Congress authorized a Congressional Gold Medal award to Pope John Paul II, stating, "To authorize a gold medal to be awarded on behalf of the Congress to Pope John II in recognition of his many and enduring contributions to peace and religious understanding, and for other purposes. ... The Congress finds that Pope John Paul II ... is recognized in the United States and abroad as a preeminent moral authority; has dedicated his Pontificate to the freedom and dignity of every individual human being and tirelessly traveled to the far reaches of the globe as an exemplar of faith; has brought hope to millions of people all over the world oppressed by poverty, hunger, illness, and despair; transcending temporal politics, has used his moral authority to hasten the fall of godless totalitarian regimes, symbolized in the collapse of the Berlin wall; has promoted the inner peace of man as well as peace among mankind through his faith-inspired defense of justice; and has thrown open the doors of the Catholic Church, reconciling differences within Christendom as well as reaching out to the world's great religions."[53]

June 5, 2000. President Putin asked Pope John Paul II for "help in gaining Russia's political and military integration in Europe." Putin called his stop at the Vatican "a very significant visit."[54]

September 5, 2000. A thirty-six-page update from the Congregation for the Doctrine of the Faith, *"Dominus Iesus,"* rejected in unambiguous terms the notion that "one religion is as good as another," that the Catholic Church is "complementary" to other religions, and that Protestants, for example, are "churches in the proper sense."[55]

October 2000. Queen Elizabeth II, head of the church and state of England, visited Pope John Paul II and stated that she was "pleased to note the important progress that has been made in overcoming historic differences between Anglicans and Roman Catholics—as exemplified in particular by the meeting of Anglicans and Roman Catholics in Canada this year. I trust that we shall continue to advance along the path which leads to Christian unity."[56]

January 6, 2001. The Pope's apostolic letter *"Novo Millennio Ineunte"* ("At the Beginning of the New Millennium"), among other directives, emphasized the importance of Sunday as "a special day of faith, the day of the Risen Lord and of the gift of the Spirit, the true weekly Easter. . . . We do not know what the new millennium has in store for us, but we are certain that it is safe in the hands of Christ, the 'King of kings and Lord of lords' (Rev. 19:16); and precisely by celebrating his Passover not just once a year but every Sunday, the Church will continue to show to every generation the true fulcrum of history, to which the mystery of the world's origin and its final destiny leads."[57]

January 31, 2001. President Bush told twenty-five Catholic leaders that his interest was to "draw on Catholic wisdom and experience. . . . I think you are seeing a historic and ground-breaking moment in the participation of Catholics in public life." Archbishop Chaput, present for the dialogue, said Catholic social teaching is based on two pillars: dignity of the individual and commitment to the common good. Bush had often referred to the "common good" as an important administrative goal.[58]

March 22, 2001. The Pope John Paul II Cultural Center opened in Washington D.C. The center was first proposed for Krakow, Warsaw, or Rome, but the Pope chose Washington, D.C., which he described as "the crossroads of the world."[59] "Cardinal Maida said there was no illusion that putting the center in Washington would precipitate an immediate change in the thinking of presidents, Supreme Court Justices, Members of Congress or other officials. . . . But as we tell the story better, people will be affected by osmosis."[60]

May 2001. John Paul II, the first Catholic leader to enter the Umayyad Mosque in the Syrian capital of Damascus, participated in an organized prayer service. For Muslims, it is the oldest stone mosque in the world, while for Christians, it is the alleged place where John the Baptist was buried. The Pope led in Christian prayers, while his Moslem counterpart, Sheikh Ahmed Kataro, led in Muslim prayers. By this dramatic act of worshiping in a mosque, the Pope underlined his commitment to work toward a rapprochement with the Muslims.

September 2001. In Almaty, Kazakhstan, twelve days after the horrors of September 11, 2001, the Pope renewed his commitment to work toward a new partnership with Muslims in his message to the predominantly Muslim nation of Kazakhstan. The Pope declared. " 'There is one God.' The Apostle proclaims before all else the absolute oneness of God. This is a truth which Christians inherited from the children of Israel and which they share with Muslims: it is faith in the one God, 'Lord of heaven and earth' (Lk.10:21), almighty and merciful. In the name of this one God, I turn to the people of deep and ancient religious traditions, the people of Kazakhstan."[61]

The Pope then appealed to both Muslims and Christians to work together to build a "civilization of love." "This 'logic of love' is what he [Jesus] holds out to us, asking us to live it above all through generosity to those in need. It is a logic that can bring together Christians and Muslims, and commit them to work together for the 'civilization of love.' It is a logic which overcomes all the cunning of this world and allows us to make true friends who will welcome us 'into the eternal dwelling-places' (Lk.16:9), into the 'homeland' of heaven."

January 24, 2002. In Assisi, Italy, the Pope and more than a hundred religious leaders from around the world, including Orthodox patriarchs, Jewish rabbis, grand muftis, sheikhs, other Muslim representatives, Buddhist and Shinto monks, Hindu leaders, Zoroastrians whose adherents are mostly in India and Iran, leaders of traditional African religions, Protestant leaders, and twenty-five Roman Catholic cardinals and approximately thirty bishops shared in a day pursuing "authentic peace." Ending the day, the Pope lit a symbolic lamp of peace with the words "Violence never again! War never again! Terrorism never again! In God's name, may all religions bring upon earth justice and peace, forgiveness, life, and love."[62]

October 16, 2003. In celebrating Pope John Paul II's twenty-five years as leader of the Roman Catholic Church, Tracy Wilkinson of the *Los Angeles Times* wrote, "This planet now is a very different place [compared to October 16, 1978], and John Paul II . . . has had a hand in shaping events to a degree unrivaled by any other religious figure in modern history. His election on Oct. 16, 1978 'was itself a breaker of precedents,' the Jesuit magazine *America* said in an editorial this month, 'and ever since his election John Paul II's pontificate has been setting records that none of his predecessors could have imagined.' "[63]

April 2, 2005. Pope John Paul II died after holding "the chair of St. Peter" for twenty-six years. He had appeared on the cover of *Time* magazine more than any other person—sixteen times. President George W. Bush made the following statement: "Laura and I join people across the earth in mourning the passing of Pope John Paul II. The Catholic Church has lost its shepherd, the world has lost a champion of human freedom, and a good and faithful servant of God has been called home."

President Bush then issued an executive order that the flag of the United States, "as a mark of respect for His Holiness, Pope John Paul II," be flown at half staff on all federal government buildings through the United States and its territories until sunset of his interment. This order included all United States embassies and other facilities abroad as well as all naval vessels.

Pope John Paul II's funeral

At John Paul II's funeral, three United States presidents knelt with bowed heads for about five minutes in front of the Pope's casket. More than a hundred official delegations also attended, including four kings, five queens, and more than seventy prime ministers. More than seven hundred thousand people rubbed shoulders in St. Peter's Square during the three-hour ceremony. On the streets of Rome, an estimated four million pilgrims watched the funeral on large screens. Around the world, it is estimated that more than two billion people watched the funeral in stadiums, churches, and private homes. It was the largest funeral in the history of the world! And analysts say that it was the largest gathering of world leaders ever!

This remarkable event was a rare display of religious plurality, attended by mourners of many religious persuasions wearing Arab head scarves, Jewish scull caps, Central Asian lambskin hats, and black veils.

Pope Benedict XVI continues Pope John Paul's agenda

And now Pope Benedict XVI, Pope John Paul's most trusted companion, will continue with even sharper voice the strongest statements regarding the importance of Sunday throughout the world. (Indeed, he may well have written his predecessor's strong messages regarding Sunday importance.)

The present Pontiff argues a concept to which Hindus, Buddhists, Muslims, and Christians will have a difficult time objecting: The Catholic Church is primarily concerned with the universal moral values based in the nature of mankind—and the Catholic Church will control the meaning of "universal" and "moral." This meaning is wrapped up in how the Church defines "natural law." From finding agreement first in "natural law" (which seems easy today), it is only a half-step to accepting Sunday as a day of rest for all in the world—in the interest of the inalienable rights of all mankind.

Speaking to a group of Polish bishops, Pope Benedict XVI built this case and then said, "It is very important, especially where a pluralistic society prevails, that there be a correct notion of the relationship between the political community and the Church and a clear distinction between the tasks which Christians undertake, individually or as a group, on their own responsibility as citizens guided by the dictates of a Christian conscience, and the activities which, in union with their pastors, they carry out in the name of the Church."[64]

What does the Pope mean? He means that no other standard of right and wrong can be used outside the pronouncements of the

Roman Catholic Church. The Pope went on to say that Catholic politicians "must take action against any form of injustice and tyranny, against domination by an individual or a political party and any intolerance."[65]

We remember that the papacy boasts "that she never changes."[66] But we have not been left to wonder how the future will unfold:

> We have been "warned of the impending danger; . . . and the Protestant world will learn what the purposes of Rome really are, only when it is too late to escape the snare. She is silently growing into power. Her doctrines are exerting their influence in legislative halls, in the churches, and in the hearts of men. She is piling up her lofty and massive structures in the secret recesses of which her former persecutions will be repeated. Stealthily and unsuspectedly she is strengthening her forces to further her own ends when the time shall come for her to strike. All that she desires is vantage ground, and this is already being given her. We shall soon see and shall feel what the purpose of the Roman element is. Whoever shall believe and obey the word of God will thereby incur reproach and persecution.[67]

Where is all this leading?

In this overview of the resurgence of the Roman Catholic Church, we can see the beginning of the fulfillment of the predictions in Revelation chapters 13–18. We now can see more clearly the end game that will usher in the framework for the fulfilling of Revelation 17:13, when the nations of earth with "one mind" will give their powers and authority to the power represented by the "beast." The global powers recognized as the United States and the papacy join in common interests, with "one mind."

For some, such a scenario is far-fetched. But for those who have been watching and listening carefully for the last forty years, the first question is not "if," but "when" and "how soon"? And the second is, What will be the catalyst that will join these two "super powers" in becoming "one mind"?

Let's briefly review certain developments of the last forty years. We have only a small space in this chapter to unfold several observations.

A new world order

Many remember President George Herbert Walker Bush's State of the Union address before the U.S. Congress on January 29, 1991.[68] A few days before, Congress had voted for war against Iraq. In his speech, Bush said, "What is at stake is more than one small country, it is a big idea—*a new world order*, where diverse nations are drawn together in common cause to achieve the universal aspirations of mankind: peace and security, freedom, and the rule of law. Such is a world worthy of our struggle, and worthy of our children's future!"

A "new world order"! For many Americans, that sounded like something describing millennial bliss! However, the phrase *new world order* has been used thousands of times in the last century by highly placed leaders in education, industry, banking, the media, and politics. Just to go down the list would make another book. In a special way, the phrase became the mantra during the decades from 1960 to 1980 for those pushing "values clarification" and "outcome-based education"—a veritable hurricane shift in the public school system's morality code in the United States.

On July 26, 1962, Nelson Rockefeller pledged in his run for the U.S. presidency that "as President, he would work toward international creation of a *new world order*." In 1968, Rockefeller published his book *The Future of Federalism*, a compelling outline of what he envisioned by a *new world order*—that the old order is crumbling and there is a "new and free order struggling to be born." He went on to say that at present there was a fever of nationalism ... [but] the nation-state is becoming less and less competent to perform its international political tasks. ... These are some of the reasons pressing us to lead vigorously toward the true building of a *new world order* ... [with] voluntary service ... and our dedicated faith in the brotherhood of all mankind. ... Sooner perhaps than we may realize ... there will evolve the basis for a federal structure of the free world (emphasis added).

In 1975, thirty-two Senators and ninety-two Representatives signed "A Declaration of Interdependence," written by the distinguished historian Henry Steele Commager, that stated, "We must join with others to bring forth a *new world order.* ... Narrow notions of national sovereignty must not be permitted to curtail that obligation."

In his address to the United Nations on December 7, 1988, Mikhail Gorbachev called for mutual consensus: "World progress is only possible through a search for universal human consensus as we move toward a *new world order.*"

On May 12, 1989, President George H. W. Bush stated that the United States is ready to welcome the Soviet Union "back into the *world order.*"

On September 11, 1990, months before the Gulf War began, President Bush emphasized his strategy: "The crisis in the Persian Gulf offers a rare opportunity to move toward an historic period of cooperation. Out of these troubled times ... *a new world order* can emerge in which the nations of the world, east and west, north and south, can prosper and live in harmony. ... Today the *new world* is struggling to be born."

A remarkable peek into how all this gets circulated into the bloodstream of Americans was revealed by David Rockefeller at the Council on Foreign Relations in June 1991. Sixty-five prestigious members of government, labor, academia, the media, military, and the professions from nine countries heard Rockefeller say,

We are grateful to the *Washington Post, The New York Times, Time* magazine, and other great publications whose directors have attended our meetings and respected their promises of discretion for almost 40 years. It would have been impossible for us to develop our plan for the world if we had been subjected to the lights of publicity during those years. But the world is now more sophisticated and prepared to march towards a world government. The supranational sovereignty of an intellectual elite and world bankers is surely preferable to the national auto-determination practiced in past centuries.[69]

It might take a couple of deep breaths and several re-reads of that paragraph to grasp what Rockefeller is revealing.

As if on cue, *Time* magazine published on July 20, 1992, Strobe Talbott's *The Birth of the Global Nation*, in which he wrote, "All countries are basically social arrangements. . . . No matter how permanent or even sacred they may seem at any one time, in fact they are all artificial and temporary. . . . Perhaps national sovereignty wasn't such a great idea after all. . . . But it has taken the events in our own wondrous and terrible century to clinch the case for world government."

Talbott was soon appointed as the number-two person in the U. S. State Department, behind Warren Christopher, where he continued his sharp focus.

Global governance

The State of the World Forum, in the fall of 1995, held its meeting at the Presidio in San Francisco attended by the who's who of the world, including Margaret Thatcher, Maurice Strong, George H. W. Bush, and Mikhail Gorbachev. *The term* global governance *was now being used instead of* new world order.

A year later, the United Nations published a four hundred twenty–page report, *Our Global Neighborhood,* that laid out the plans for "global governance" in the years ahead.

The point is, it might be taking somewhat longer than first thought to achieve the "new world" dream that key world leaders have been working on behind the scenes for decades. But the trajectory has never been sharper than today. One has to be blind and deaf not to detect its forward motion in politics, social programs, and financial enterprises, as well as in religious confederations never thought possible a generation ago.

Rise of the future pope

But the "new world order" strategy has its mirror image, a linkage that will soon become more evident. This parallel movement found enormous traction in the rise of Pope John II, beginning even before he became the 263rd successor to Peter the Apostle, as Catholics would call it.

Now we can see more clearly what the Polish arcbishop from Krakow meant in 1976 when he said, "We are now standing in the face of the greatest historical confrontation humanity has gone through . . . a test of 2,000 years of culture and Christian civilization, with all of its consequences for human dignity, individual rights, and the rights of nations." But, he continued, "Wide circles of American society and wide circles of the Christian community do not realize this fully."[70]

Of course, the soon-to-be pope was speaking of the three major global powers that sooner or later would meld into one—the Soviet Union under Mikhail Gorbachev, the United States led by Ronald Reagan, and the most deeply experienced of the major powers, the papacy.[71] Each, in their time and continued today in their successors, had the same geopolitical aims; each had a grand design for world governance "that will replace the decaying nation system."

As a few short years passed, the grand design in the mind of Gorbachev faded, leaving only two world powers to lead the inexorable flow of "the new world order." But, from the beginning of his pontificate in October 1978, Pope John Paul II astonished the world with his decision to become a decisive factor in determining the "new world order." He did it without press agents or a clever propaganda machine; he did it himself. In his first twelve years, he made forty-five papal trips to ninety-one countries, giving a total of 1,559 speeches in thirty-two languages, being heard in the flesh or on audio-video hookups by more than 3.5 billion people.[72]

But what is even more astonishing is that Pope John Paul II never traveled as a casual tourist or a distinguished visitor. Hardly! He was formally received by the host government in a category far above a Billy Graham or Dalai Lama or any other religious leader. One hundred twenty governments sent diplomatic missions to his Vatican home Every comment on his thoughts and acts was front-page news. And no government complained or tried to argue with him. No one gave him the right to speak as religious authority on all things political and moral—he simply assumed it.

He was always cementing these international relationships, yet always waiting—for what? He had been waiting

for an event that will fission human history, splitting the immediate past from the oncoming future. It will be an event on public view in the skies, in the oceans, and on the continental landmasses of this planet. It will particularly involve our human sun, which every day lights up and shines upon the valleys, the mountains and the plains of this earth for our eyes. But on the day of this event, it will not appear merely as the master star of our so-called solar system. Rather, it will be seen as the circumambient glory of the Woman whom the apostle describes as "clothed with the sun" and giving birth to "a child who will rule the nations with a scepter of iron."[73]

One of the driving forces in Pope John Paul's life was that he took the Fatima[74] message personally. He believed that he was designated God's servant in the divine plan and providence, that he had an unpleasant message and, perhaps, a thankless job. He strongly felt that he had to warn the world of his conviction that human catastrophe on a world scale was impending. However, he knew it would not come without a warning, but that only those with renewed hearts would "recognize it for what it is and make preparations for the tribulations that will follow."[75]

In this, we can see the beginning of the fulfillment of the predictions in Revelation chapters 13–18; now we see more clearly the end game that will usher in the framework for the fulfilling of Revelation 17:13, when the nations of earth with "one mind" will give their power and authority to the power represented by the "beast." The global power recognized as the United States and the global power recognized as the papacy join in common interests, with "one mind."

In the light of all these events, how remarkable, how precise was Ellen White's prediction:

The so-called Christian world is to be the theater of great and decisive actions. Men in authority will enact laws controlling the conscience, after the example of the papacy. Babylon will make all nations drink of the wine of the wrath of her fornication. Every nation will be involved. Of this time John the Revelator declares:

"The merchants of the earth are waxed rich through the abundance of her delicacies. And I heard another voice from heaven, saying, Come out of her, my people, that ye be not partakers of her sins, and that ye receive not of her plagues. For her sins have reached unto heaven, and God hath remembered her iniquities. Reward her even as she rewarded you, and double unto her double according to her works: in the cup which she hath filled fill to her double. How much she hath glorified herself, and lived deliciously, so much torment and sorrow give her: for she saith in her heart, I sit a queen, and am no widow, and shall see no sorrow" (Rev. 18:3–7).

"These have one mind, and shall give their power and strength unto the beast. These shall make war with the Lamb, and the Lamb shall overcome them: for he is Lord of lords, and King of kings: and they that are with him are called, and chosen, and faithful" (Rev. 17:13, 14).

"These have one mind." There will be a universal bond of union, one great harmony, a confederacy of Satan's forces. "And shall give their power and strength unto the beast." Thus is manifested the same arbitrary, oppressive power against religious liberty, freedom to worship God according to the dictates of conscience, as was manifested by the papacy, when in the past it persecuted those who dared to refuse to conform with the religious rites and ceremonies of Romanists.[76]

The apostle Peter adds, "We also have the prophetic word made more sure, which you do well to heed as a light that shines in a dark place, until the day dawns and the morning star rises in your hearts" (2 Peter 1:19).

---

1. Ellen G. White, *The Spirit of Prophecy* (Oakland, Calif.: Pacific Press® Publishing Association, 1884), 4:390.

2. E. G. White, *Testimonies for the Church*, 5:451 (see chap. 1, n. 5).

3. Ellen G. White, *Review and Herald*, June 1, 1886.

4. E. G. White, *The Great Controversy*, 581 (see chap. 2, n. 10).

5. Ibid., 563.

6. Ibid.

7. Ibid., 566.

8. Ibid.

9. Ibid., 567.

10. Ibid., 571.

11. Ibid.

12. Ibid., 572.

13. For papal influence on the development of a Sunday law in the United States, see the next chapter in this book.

14. E. G. White, *The Great Controversy*, 573.

15. Ellen G. White Comments, *Seventh-day Adventist Bible Commentary* (Washington, D.C.: 1980), 7:975.

16. E. G. White, *The Great Controversy*, 578.

17. Ibid., 579.

18. Ibid., 580.

19. Ibid., 581.

20. Ibid. In January 2001, of the 535 members of the 107th U.S. Congress, 150 were Roman Catholic; there were 72 Baptists, 65 Methodists, 49 Presbyterians, 41 Episcopalians, 37 Jews, 20 Lutherans, 15 Mormons, plus others.—PCUSA.NEWS@ ecunet.org January 9, 2001. In 2005, Roman Catholics in Congress numbered 152, or 29 percent.

21. Malachi Martin, *The Keys of This Blood* (New York: Simon & Schuster, 1990), 16.

22. See David A.Yallop, *In God's Name: An Investigation into the Murder of Pope John Paul I* (New York: Bantam Books, 1984).

23. *U. S. News and World Report*, October 30, 1978.

24. "No attempt would have been made to cut him down so early in his pontificate if indeed as a spiritual leader he represented no political threat into those who ordered his assassination. The present Dalai Lama, the archbishop of Canterbury, or Billy Graham are not likely to undergo a like fate. They don't matter, as John Paul matters."—Malachi Martin, *The Decline and Fall of the Roman Church* (New York: G. P. Putnam's Sons, 1981), 294. See also Martin, *Keys of This Blood*, 46.

25. *Time*, February 24, 1992, 28.

26. Pope John Paul II "insists that men have no reliable hope of creating a viable geopolitical system unless it is on the basis of Roman Catholic Christianity."—Martin, *Keys of This Blood*, 492.

27. Thomas P. Melady, *The Ambassador's Story—The United States and the Vatican in World Affairs* (Huntington, Ind.: Our Sunday Visitor, Inc., 1994), 50.

28. Ibid., 491.

29. *South Bend Tribune*, March 9, 1992, cited in Dwight K. Nelson, *Countdown to the Showdown* (Fallbrook, Calif.: Hart Research Center, 1992), 40, 41.

30. *Life*, December 1989.

31. *Time*, December 4, 1989.

32. (New York: Simon & Schuster, 1990).

33. Pope John Paul II, *"Centesimus Annus,"* http://www.ewtn.com/library/ENCYC/JP2HUNDR.HTM.

34. *Time*, February 24, 1992, 24–35.

35. Alan Cowell in the *New York Times*, August 18, 1993.

36. *National Catholic Register*, January 9, 16, 1994.

37. The full text of the document is found in Clifford Goldstein's *One Nation Under God?* (Nampa, Idaho: Pacific Press® Publishing Association, 1996), 143–160. See "Catholics and Evangelicals in the Trenches," *Christianity Today*, May 16, 1994; J. I. Packer, "Why I Signed It," *Christianity Today*, December 12, 1994.

38. John White, former president of the National Association of Evangelicals, *USA TODAY*, March 30, 1994. On March 29, 1994, *The Oregonian* summarized an Associated Press story with the subtitle "Catholic and evangelical leaders vow to join in a common bond to work toward shared values."

39. *National Catholic Register*, October 16, 1994.

40. *National Catholic Register*, December 11, 1994.

41. *Christianity Today*, November 14, 1994. One of the books I read in my early ministry was Paul Blanchard's *American Freedom and Catholic Power* (Boston: The Beacon Press, 1949). A breathtaking book, it reveals how the Catholic Church would eventually dominate the politics of the United States, long before others were writing with such precision. How would they do this? The church would turn the eyes of conservative Protestant America toward common values such as birth control, abortion, family values, and control of education. In that same year, America saw a very effective advertising campaign sponsored by the Knights of Columbus to remove misconceptions about Rome.

42. December 26, 1994 /January 2, 1995, 53, 54.

43. *The Orlando Sentinel,* January 22, 1995.

44. *"Ut Unum Sint,"* http://www.vatican.va/edocs/ENG0221/_INDEX.HTM. Richard John Neuhaus, *The Wall Street Journal*, July 6, 1995.

45. Joseph L. Conn, "Papal Blessing?" *Church and State*, November, 1995.

46. John Paul II, *"Dies Domini,"* http://www.vatican.va/holy_father/john_paul_ii/apost_letters/documents/hf_jp-ii_apl_05071998_dies-domini_en.html.

47. "Discorso di S.E. Mons. Jean-Louis Tauran Sui Papporti Tra La Santa Sede E Gerusalemme, 26.10.1998," http://212.77.1.245/news_services/bulletin/news/3824.php?index=3824&po_date=26.10.1998%20%20&lang=ge.

48. Associated Press, 10/30/98 1:12, PM.

49. This "Statement from the Co-Chairmen of the Anglican-Roman Catholic International Commission" can be found in its entirety on the Vatican Web site, http://www.vatican.va/roman_curia/pontifical_councils/chrstuni/documents/rc_pc_chrstuni_doc_12051999_gift-of-autority_en.html. John Wilkins, editor of

The Tablet, commented: "This 'Gift of Authority' now joins the other documents developed by this conference as an agenda in waiting. The commission's work is like a deposit in a bank. Its value will be evident when the time comes for it to be withdrawn for us." "Anglican-Catholic Commission Reaches Agreement on Authority, *National Catholic Reporter* Online, http://natcath.org/NCR_Online/archives2/1999b/060499/060499l.htm. Dr. George Carey, archbishop of Canterbury said, "In a world torn apart by violence and division, Christians need urgently to be able to speak with a common voice, confident of the authority of the gospel of peace."—Oliver Poole, "Churches Agree Pope Has Overall Authority," BBC News.

50. ZENIT, March 12, 13, 2000. "John Paul has one foot in the dimension of history (where mess, error, violence, fanaticism and stupidity flourish merrily) and the other in the dimension of eternity (where he must insist, the holiness and infallibility of the church as the mystical body of Christ remain intact). It is awkward: How does infallibility own up to its fallibilities and yet remain infallible? The Pope's solution: by being vague about the actual sins and by attributing them, in any case, to men and women who are Catholics and not to the Catholic Church itself."—Lance Morrow, "Is it Enough to Be Sorry?" *Time,* March 27, 2000.

51. *Christianity Today,* October 25, 1999.

52. Associated Press, November 8, 1999.

53. Test of the Pope John Paul II Congressional Gold Medal Act as introduced in the House of Representatives can be seen at http://thomas.loc.gov/. Search 108th Congress for John Paul II.

54. CNN.com. June 5, 2000.

55. Catholic World News—Vatican Updates—09/05/2000; *Christianity Today,* September 11, 2000.

56. "17 Oct 2000 – Address Presented by The Queen to His Holines The Pope at The Vatican," http://www.etoile.co.uk/Speech/RomePope2000.html.

57. Apostolic letter *"Novo Millennio Inuente,"* http://www.vatican.va/holy _father/john_paul_ii/apost_letters/documents/hf_jp-ii_apl_20010106 _novo-millennio-ineunte_en.html.

58. "Bush Meets With Catholics on Faith-based Initiatives," *National Catholic Register,* February 11–17, 2001.

59. Pat McCloskey, "Washington's New Pope John Paul II Cultural Center," *St. Anthony Messenger,* April 2001.

60. *The National Catholic Register,* October 26–November 1, 1997.

61. Homily of the Holy Father, "Pilgrimage to Kazakhstan," http://www .vatican.va/holy_father/john_paul_ii/homilies/2001/documents/hf_jp-ii_hom _20010923_kazakhstan_astana_en.html.

62. *Christian Science Monitor,* January 24, 2002; "Pope hosts ecumenical assembly for peace at Assisi," INQ7.net, January 24, 2002.

63. *The Sacramento Bee,* October 16, 2003.

64. ZENIT, December 18, 2005. I am indebted to Marcus Sheffield.

65. Ibid.

66. E. G. White, *The Great Controversy*, 581.

67. Ibid.

68. The Associated Press.

69. Nelson Rockefeller, *The Future of Federalism* (Cambridge, Mass.: Harvard University Press, 1962).

70. Martin, *Keys of This Blood*, 16.

71. Ibid., 17. Martin observed that the "final contender in the competition for the new world order is not a single individual leader or a single institution or territory. It is a group of men who are united as one in power, mind and will for the purpose of achieving a single common goal: to be victorious in the competition for the new global hegemony."—17.

72. Ibid., 490.

73. Ibid., 639.

74. On October 13, 1917, three peasant girls claimed they saw and heard Mary, our Lord's mother, who gave them three messages. The first two messages were soon revealed, but the third was not to be opened until 1960. The first put the church, as well as society in general, on notice that they were heading toward the eternal punishment of hell. The second is understood as a prophecy of World War II and that Russia would spread evil throughout the world and that many would suffer and die. The third message, written by the surviving child who became a Carmelite nun in Coimbra, Portugal, was opened by John XXIII who felt it had no relevance to his pontificate, so it was returned to its hiding place in the Pope's quarters until Pope John Paul II made it available. The message referred to physical and spiritual chastisement of the nations of the world, including Roman Catholics—all of which may be mitigated by prayers to "Mother Mary."—Ibid., 627–233.

75. Ibid., 637.

76. E. G. White, *Selected Messages*, 3:392 (see chap. 2, n. 3).

Chapter Six

THE HARDEST PREDICTION TO BELIEVE—THE UNITED STATES IN END TIME

One of the most amazing predictions of the mid-nineteenth century appeared in the May 1851 issue of the *Review and Herald* written by twenty-two-year-old John N. Andrews of Paris, Maine. It launched a line of thought that has become increasingly relevant as time has continued, but when Andrews wrote that the fledgling United States—barely seventy-five years old at that time—would become a world superpower, nothing could have seemed more unimaginable.

Andrews based his prediction on his study of Revelation 13:11–18. Reviewing the major world powers predicted in the book of Daniel and the historical fulfillment of the outline given there, Andrews noted that each of the world empires were "ever tending westward" and that following this trend, "we still look westward for the rise of the power described in this prophecy [Revelation 13:11–18]."

Young Andrews did his homework, quoting a current magazine article: "In the west an opposing and still more wonderful American empire is EMERGING." He carefully noted the biblical features of the young country that he saw symbolized in Revelation by the beast with lamblike horns. For Andrews, these two horns denoted the "civil and religious power of this nation—its Republican civil power, and its Protestant ecclesiastical power."

Further in the article, he observed, "It is of itself a wonder, a system of government which has not its like elsewhere. . . . The two-horned beast is from the time of the rise a power contemporary with the first beast [papal Rome], and not the first beast in another form." Andrews goes on to identify this two-horned power as the United States of America and to predict, based on the prophecy, a coming showdown between seventh-day Sabbath keepers and those enforcing the "the mark of the beast" through the power of the United States.

This is heady reading *today*! For most of those living in the 1850s, this kind of thinking must have seemed far-fetched and delusional. Think about it. The population of this young country was less than twenty-four million. California, the thirty-first state, had been admitted to the Union only the year before Andrews wrote his article in the *Review and Herald*. A hundred-acre wheat field remained the limit that any one man could farm. In 1850, the first Singer sewing machine was patented. Kerosene and the safety elevator had not yet been invented, a railroad from the East had not yet reached Chicago, and oil had not yet been discovered. Compulsory school attendance was not yet law. To think that this young nation, sparsely populated and mostly agricultural expanse, would become a world superpower defied credibility!

Why was Andrews so positive about identifying the "two-horned" beast of Revelation 13 as the United States? Obviously, not because of what he read in his current newspaper! Young Andrews was reading his Bible! He may also have had access to historical records that had been linking the papacy with the first beast of Revelation 13 for several centuries.[1] There was some precedent for Andrews's position. Prior to his May 1851 article, three Sabbatarian Adventists (the Sabbath-keeping Adventists had not yet formally assumed the name Seventh-day Adventists), George W. Holt, Hiram Edson, and H. S. Case, had linked the two horns of the beast described in Revelation 13 with civil and ecclesiastical power.[2]

Now we can understand the validity in Ellen White's comment in 1888:

> For about forty years, students of prophecy in the United States have presented this testimony to the world. In the events now taking place is seen a rapid advance toward the fulfillment of the prediction. With Protestant teachers there is the same claim of divine authority for Sunday-keeping, and the same lack of scriptural evidence, as with the papist leaders who fabricated miracles to supply the place of a command from God. The assertion that God's judgments are visited upon men for their violation of the Sunday-sabbath, will be repeated; already it is beginning to be urged. And a movement to enforce Sunday observance is fast gaining ground.[3]

What we have here is an example of how Ellen White used historians known for their biblical scholarship, past and contemporary, to gather details filling in her broad unfolding of the great controversy between God and Satan. Her prophetic insights confirmed the biblical argument that Andrews expressed so eloquently in his article of May 1851. But with prophetic insight, she saw more:

> When Protestantism shall stretch her hand across the gulf to grasp the hand of the Roman power, when she shall reach over the abyss to clasp hands with Spiritualism, when, under the influence of this threefold union, our country shall repudiate every principle of its Constitution as a Protestant and republican government, and shall make provision for the propagation of papal falsehoods and delusions, then we may know that the time has come for the marvelous working of Satan and that the end is near.[4]

When the leading churches of the United States, uniting upon such points of doctrine as are held by them in common, shall influence the state to enforce their decrees and to sustain their institutions, then Protestant America will have formed an image of the Roman hierarchy, and the infliction of civil penalties upon dissenters will inevitably result.[5]

The Protestants of the United States will be foremost in stretching their hands across the gulf to grasp the hand of Spiritualism; they will reach over the abyss to clasp hands with the Roman power; and under the influence of this threefold union, this country will follow in the steps of Rome in trampling on the rights of conscience.[6]

The beast with two horns is also to say "to them that dwell on the earth, that they should make an image to the beast;" and, furthermore, it is to command all, "both small and great, rich and poor, free and bond," to receive the mark of the beast. Revelation 13:11-16. It has been shown that the United States is the power represented by the beast with lamblike horns, and that this prophecy will be fulfilled when the United States shall enforce Sunday observance, which Rome claims as the special acknowledgment of her supremacy.[7]

Political corruption is destroying love of justice and regard for truth; and even in free America, rulers and legislators, in order to secure public favor, will yield to the popular demand for a law enforcing Sunday observance. Liberty of conscience, which has cost so great a sacrifice, will no longer be respected. In the soon-coming conflict we shall see exemplified the prophet's words: "The dragon was wroth with the woman, and went to make war with the remnant of her seed, which keep the commandments of God, and have the testimony of Jesus Christ." Revelation 12:17.[8]

A time is coming when the law of God is, in a special sense, to be made void in our land. The rulers of our nation will, by legislative enactments, enforce the Sunday law, and thus God's people be brought into great peril. When our nation, in its legislative councils, shall enact laws to bind the consciences of men in regard to their religious privileges, enforcing Sunday observance, and bringing oppressive power to bear against those who keep the seventh-day Sabbath, the law of God will, to all intents and purposes, be made void in our land; and national apostasy will be followed by national ruin.[9]

The people of the United States have been a favored people; but when they restrict religious liberty, surrender Protestantism, and give countenance to popery, the measure of their guilt will be full, and "national apostasy" will be registered in the books of heaven. The result of this apostasy will be national ruin.[10]

As America, the land of religious liberty, shall unite with the papacy in forcing the conscience and compelling men to honor the false sabbath, the people of every country on the globe will be led to follow her example.[11]

The less we make direct charges against authorities and powers, the greater work we shall be able to accomplish, both America and in foreign countries. Foreign nations will follow the example of the United States. Though she leads out, yet the same crisis will come upon our people in all parts of the world.[12]

What does all this mean? In a quick overview, we note several events that will happen in rapid succession:

- Protestants of the United States stretch across the gulf to join hands with spiritualism and over the abyss to clasp hands with the papacy; under this threefold union, this country will follow in the steps of Rome in trampling on the rights of conscience.
- Leading churches of the United States unite upon doctrines or values held in common, influencing the government to enforce their decrees and to sustain their institutions; thus Protestant America will form an image of the papacy.
- Revelation 13 will be fulfilled when the United States enforces Sunday observance, which Rome claims as the acknowledgment of her supremacy.
- Political corruption will destroy love of justice and regard for truth in free America; rulers and legislators, in order to secure public favor, will yield to the popular demand for enforcing Sunday observance. Liberty of conscience will no longer be respected.
- The United States will repudiate its Constitution as a Protestant and republican government.
- Countries all over the earth will follow the example of the United States in exalting the religious leadership of the papacy and in enacting worldwide Sunday laws.
- National apostasy will be followed by national ruin.

Does any of this sound like someone's delusional conspiracy theory? What do we see in our daily newspapers and round-the-clock TV news channels? Is there anything far-fetched in Ellen White's description of the end time in the United States? Is there anything in her description of the United States in the last days that sounds like a mere projection of what she observed in the nineteenth century? Does her emphasis on truth—that it should be honored, cherished, and protected—sound passé and outmoded in our "progressive," politically correct, and tolerant twenty-first century?

Protestants and Catholics unite on common doctrines

In March 1994, forty prominent religious leaders formulated a document titled "Evangelicals and Catholics Together: The Christian Mission in the Third Millennium." It could easily be argued that in doing
so, they reversed five hundred years of church history. To imply, in the
document, that both sides preach the same Christ, understand authority and the "church" in the same way, or hold the same understanding of "justification by grace through faith" is a test of credulity.
Yet both sides agree to uphold "sanctity of life, family values, parental
choice in education, moral standards in society, and democratic institutions worldwide." The document states further, "We affirm that a
common set of core values is found in the teachings of religions, and
that these form the basis of a global ethic . . . and which are the conditions for a sustainable world order." New phrases such as the church
being responsible "for the right ordering of civil society" are more
than interesting. The document goes on to say that "it is neither theologically legitimate nor a prudent use of resources" to proselytize
among active members of another Christian community.

Would Martin Luther or any of the other Reformers have said, as
does this document, that "Evangelicals and Catholics are brothers and
sisters in Christ"?

These prominent religious leaders unitedly affirmed that Evangelicals and Catholics should stand together to oppose abortion and pornography and to share the common values of honesty, observance of
law, work, caring, chastity, mutual respect between the sexes, parent-
hood, and family. And, yes, they contend that "Christians individually
and the church corporately also have a responsibility for the right ordering of civil society."

This "right ordering of civil society" fails to distinguish between
legislating morality in the area of human freedom and laws that govern how one worships the God of morality. It seems to me that "religious" legislation in the end time will come under the guise of laws

that will address social crises—a smooth way to segue into "rational" reasons to unite for the "common good."[13]

Further, as these two religious forces, Evangelicals and Roman Catholics, unite in common cause, pursuing the common good, they will prod legislative assemblies to enforce their decrees and to sustain their institutions which, in essence, is a repeat of papal history when for centuries the church used the state to sustain and enforce its religious programs. This repetition of history Ellen White calls "an image of the Roman hierarchy," a mirror reflection of centuries of church-state union—and its appalling consequences.

The result of this civil enforcement of religious decrees will be the "infliction of civil penalties upon dissenters." A national crisis of any kind would make this document of common values a clarion call for all those who hold these common values to rise up in unprecedented national unity—a unity framed in legislation.

Political corruption leads to popular demands

Ellen White predicted that political corruption would destroy love of justice and eventually lead to the popular demand for the enforcement of a Sunday law. For most people, this prediction has seemed absurd; surely, nothing like this could happen in a country that reveres the First Amendment to its Constitution!

It all depends on definitions.

For the Supreme Court today to affirm a national Sunday law as a special religious day seems highly unlikely. But the same Court could easily act on precedent and support the contention that Sunday is the most likely day in the week to promote neighborhood and national unity on "common values."

For years, the Supreme Court has used its "Lemon test" to determine church-state relationships. The test requires that a law must have a secular purpose and not advance or hinder the interests of any religion.

But the Supreme Court is not above reversing itself, depending on shifts toward the right or left of the worldviews of the justices. Religious freedom in the United States is wonderful theory, but the applications of that theory depend on the subjective presuppositions of a changeable court.

For instance, Americans' constitutional protections were eclipsed after the Japanese attack on Pearl Harbor, December 7, 1941. The imprisonment of approximately 120,000 Americans of Japanese heritage, young and old, proved that in times of national crisis, such protections were nonexistent—all in response to public opinion.

In this case, when the Supreme Court upheld the actions of Congress and the executive arm, Justice Robert Jackson wrote, in dissent, that the ruling was a "subtle blow to liberty. . . . The principle then lies about like a loaded weapon ready for the hand of any authority that can bring forward a plausible claim of an urgent need."[14]

Omnipotence of the majority

Alexis de Tocqueville, in his peerless analysis of American life and government, wrote that "if ever the free institutions of America are destroyed, that event may be attributed to the omnipotence of the majority, which may at some future time urge the minorities to desperation."[15]

The day is coming, sooner than almost anyone can imagine, when the majority in America will suddenly look at this country as do many foreign countries today. At a time when our government is trying to sell the American way of life worldwide, many countries are doing their best to keep us out. Why? Compared to their cultures, we look decadent and forbidding. They see our crime statistics, our flouting of sexual excess and perversion, our alcohol problems, and the extravagant portrayal of this decadence in our entertainment media. Any day now, the majority in the United States will sense that the "American Way" of today must return to the "American Way" of a century ago. Revulsion against decadence will become a national issue. The convergence of natural and economic disasters will enflame the general public with a common cry: "Something has to be done!"

The issue that will unify the majority will likely be a national day of rest. Perhaps led by the Evangelicals and Catholics, who already have joined hands, and pointing to an "urgent need," the majority will demand that legislators force some kind of national unity. Citing the biblical pronouncement that "righteousness exalteth a nation" (Proverbs 14:34), most Americans will agree that a national Sunday law would be a visible witness that the United States is pulling its moral house together.

Common "Community Day"

We are not dealing with future "maybes." In the Netherlands, on December 5, 2002, the *Nederlands Dagblads* reported that two opposing political parties voted to make Sunday a "Community Day"; however, "their ideas about such a day differ like night and day. The Christian Union asks for the closing of shops on Sundays . . . and strives to make Sunday a day of rest for everyone. By contrast, the Labor Party allows people to do whatever they like on Sunday. . . . This law, however, will cut the weekend by 50%, from the two days to only one day which will be Sunday, the only official day of rest."[16]

I can assure you that more countries will soon follow this example; a coming Sunday law in the United States is as real as the fact that the sun will rise tomorrow morning. In fact, we don't have to look far to see the groundwork already laid for a national Sunday law in the United States. In 1961, a majority ruling of the U.S. Supreme Court in *McGowan v. Maryland* upheld the constitutionality of Sunday laws even though they happened "to coincide or harmonize" with a religion! Talk about legal fiction! The Court was telling Americans that if the majority were to enjoy the benefits of a uniform day of rest, that benefit would outweigh any burden that such a law would impose on a minority group. Of course, almost anyone could see through that reasoning, *even as the dissenting judges did*. The case would not have come to the Supreme Court if religious issues were not involved! *But the majority ruled*. This 1961 ruling has cast a dark shadow forward; soon thunderclouds will roll.

Superpower United States causes the whole earth to recognize the spiritual leadership of the papacy

Revelation 13:12–14 outlines an ominous scenario: The United States has the power and influence to lead other nations into "worshiping" the papacy as the spiritual leader of the world. By means of spectacular events, or because of terrible natural disasters, the United States will dramatically grasp the attention of those that dwell on the earth and take the lead in making the papacy the linchpin in establishing world peace.

Some may ask, Does the United States really have that much world influence, and does it really want it?

Incredible as it may have sounded in the nineteenth century and for most of the twentieth century, the circumstances of the last few years have vaulted the United States into the position of being the only superpower on planet Earth. No other world power in history—not the Persian nor Roman nor Spanish nor British empires—has ever been the world's sole superpower. Today, the United States has no close competitor. For example, America spends more on its military than do the twenty countries with the next highest military expenditures! And the rest of the world expects the United States to employ its military forces to trouble spots anywhere on the globe. But far beyond its military might is America's leadership in technology, economic strength, and humanitarian relief.

With the world slipping into common talk regarding the New

World Order (or "global governance"), the thought that only America could make it happen is the world's no-brainer.

But what is so incongruous, so difficult to put together, is the fact that although the United States is admittedly the most powerful nation on earth, it is also the foremost example of a nation established on the principles of political and religious freedom! The world had never before seen a nation that has so resolutely wrapped itself within a Declaration of Independence and a Constitution that stands so clearly and forthrightly upon human rights and freedoms. The American Declaration of Independence states simply and nobly, "We hold these truths to be self-evident, that all men are created equal, and that they are endowed by their Creator with certain unalienable rights, among which are life, liberty, and the pursuit of happiness." Fifty-six heroic men signed this document and this personal commitment: "With a firm reliance on the Protection of Divine Providence, we mutually pledge to each other our Lives, our Fortunes and our sacred Honor."

Could all this change?

So how will Satan's lies and deceptions set up the United States to be the world leader in uniting all nations under a religious authority with sufficient universal clout to enforce economic hardship and persecution on those who fail to fall into line with its agenda? How will Satanic lies become so believable that the world will worship the beast (see Revelation 13:4)? I submit it will happen by

- pretense and consistent lies, though appearing to serve a noble purpose.
- blaming the national crises on those who do not follow the majority program.
- causing confusion in substituting policy for principle (the end justifies the means), substituting opinion for absolute truths, and redefining the meaning of words.

- employing various forms of coercion—and all to one end, the eradication of dissent and individual freedom.

A brief reality check

One of Pope John Paul II's primary goals was to unite the world's religions. This was expressed especially in his 1994 apostolic letter *"Tertio Millennio Adveniente"* ("The Coming Third Millennium"). This goal was even more directly detailed in his 1995 encyclical *"Ut Unum Sint"* ("That They May Be One"). And then, among other events in 2000, the United States Congress authorized a Congressional Gold Medal to be presented to Pope John Paul II in recognition of his "preeminent moral authority" and noting that in "transcending temporal politics, [he] has used his moral authority to hasten the fall of godless totalitarian regimes . . . has promoted the inner peace of man as well as peace among mankind through his faith-inspired defense of justice, and has thrown open the doors of the Catholic Church, reconciling differences within Christendom as well as reaching out to the world's great religions."

Proceeding with his global peace plan, Pope John Paul II gathered more than a hundred international religious leaders at Assisi, Italy, in 2002, pursuing "authentic peace."

Pope John Paul II made a point of wooing Mecca to Rome. He emphasized that all Christians and Muslims worship the same God, that their mutual responsibility is to build a "civilization of love," and that it is a "logic of love" that will bring all Christians and Muslims together in world peace.

All this is destined to bear fruit. The day is coming when something like the following *may* happen: Walking across the Hudson River and into the United Nations building, a religious figure (perhaps even a representation of the Virgin Mary) will galvanize world leaders buried under the weight of dozens of world conflicts. From that powerful rostrum, world delegates will hear peace plans to solve Ireland's never-ending hostility between Catholics and Protestants, proposals that will bring harmony between Israelis and Palestinians, and do the same for racial divisions in all countries. Muslims and their neighbors the world over will suddenly see a workable plan for peace. The delegates stand in unison, recognizing that this dynamic religious leader has laid out the most sensible solutions for all their problems. They can only wonder why these solutions weren't thought of before! So reasonable, so believable!

The papacy, working through these political and religious leaders, will soon have its way, breaking down all kinds of traditional international barriers as it receives the adulation of the whole world—an adulation led by the United States. Remember, "All the world marveled and followed the beast. So they worshipped the dragon [Satan] who gave authority to the beast; and they [the world] worshipped the beast, saying, 'Who is like the beast?' " Further, the two-horned beast "exercises all the authority of the first beast . . . and causes the earth and those who dwell in it to worship the first beast, whose deadly wound was healed. . . . And he deceives those who dwell on the earth . . . telling those who dwell on the earth to make an image to the beast" (Revelation 13:3, 4, 11–14).

A contrapuntal fugue

Today, almost like a contrapuntal fugue, religious leaders in the United States are unfolding the predictions of Revelation 13. On Sunday, May 17, 2006, religious leaders throughout the nation focused on Ten Commandments Day. Tens of thousands of congregations across the United States heard their pastors emphasize the importance and authority of God's law. It's hard to imagine! Strange as it may seem, Protestant and Jewish stalwarts are increasingly united in support of the relevance of the Ten Commandments—a posture that has moved 180 degrees from most of their rhetoric for more than a century. Unfortunately, however, they are not yielding to the obvious intent of the fourth commandment.

What is their driving purpose? They point to a host of disturbing trends and court actions that

> have threatened the very fabric and foundation of our culture and faith. The Ten Commandments and all other references to God, which have served as the moral foundation and anchor of our great country, are systematically being removed from public places. Public displays of the Ten Commandments and other symbols of our faith have been a powerful visual testimony to the fact that the United States of America is "one nation under God." Their removal from public places shows that those with a secular humanist agenda are intent on destroying the moral heritage of our nation. . . . The Ten Commandment Commission was founded to counter the secular agenda and help restore the Ten Commandments and Judeo-Christian values to their rightful place in our society.[17]

In his book *The New World Order,* Pat Robertson writes, "The utopians have talked of world order. Without saying so explicitly, the Ten Commandments set the only order that will bring world peace—with devotion to and respect of God at the center, strong family bonds and respect next, and the sanctity of people, property, family, reputation, and peace of mind next."[18]

In respect to the fourth commandment, the Sabbath, Robertson writes, "The next obligation that a citizen of God's world order owes is to himself. 'Remember the Sabbath day, to keep it holy,' is a command for the personal benefit of each citizen. Our minds, spirits, and bodies demand a regular time of rest. Perhaps God's greatest gift to mankind's earthly existence is the ability to be free from work one day a week."[19]

Pat Robertson is only one voice among many who are calling for the necessity and urgency of Sunday sacredness. From labor union leaders, official denominational resolutions, magazine columnists, and the papacy itself, the crescendo is developing. Note Pope John Paul II's (July 7, 1998) apostolic letter *"Dies Domini"* ("The Lord's Day").[20]

Worldwide polarization against Sabbath keepers

What seems most incredible at the moment is the prediction that there will be a *worldwide* polarization against Sabbath keepers. It almost takes one's breath away to read that when "America, the land of religious liberty, shall unite with the papacy in forcing the conscience and compelling men to honor the false sabbath, the people of every country on the globe will be led to follow her example."[21] "The Sabbath question is to be the issue in the great final conflict in which all the world will act a part."[22] A "new world order," indeed!

Yet, with great craft, the "beast" power of Revelation 13 will use the panic caused throughout the world by natural disasters, interlocking economic distress, and unsettled ethnic/religious conflicts to accomplish its long-sought goals. The prestige and power of the United States will become the model of how to unify a worldwide majority to call for God to calm earth's calamities as surely as Jesus calmed the stormy Sea of Galilee.

All of these predictions of a political/religious virus (such as the international enforcement of Sunday laws) that begins like an infection in the United States, but which will spread rapidly throughout the bloodstream of world communities—all these predictions are no longer merely a bad dream. Almost any TV talk show or weekly magazine contains references to the worldwide influence and power of the United States. When one considers that the United States selects the foreign countries that will receive billions of dollars annually in U.S. aid based on considerations of what is best for America, that terrible earthquakes and famines call forth massive U.S. humanitarian relief anywhere in the world, that the nations of the world expect the U.S.

military to resolve civil wars overseas, no one doubts any longer the clout of American opinion and action.

Since September 11, 2001, the expectation that U.S. wealth and power would be a benign security blanket for the world has morphed into the realization that *something* must be done to guarantee peace, prosperity, and the spread of human rights on every continent. Such goals in order to survive "will require the expenditure of American will and might." Condoleezza Rice, U.S. Secretary of State, when asked if the United States is "overly ambitious," replied, "Was it overly ambitious of the United States to believe that democracy could be fostered in Japan [following World War II] and that peace could finally be brought between Germany and France? It succeeded because it proceeded from values that Americans understand. Truman and his team understood that America could not afford to leave a vacuum in the world."[23]

President George H. W. Bush, in his State of the Union Address on January 29, 1991, announced, "For two centuries, we've done the hard work of freedom. And tonight, we lead the world in facing down a threat to decency and humanity. What is at stake is more than one small country; it is a big idea: a new world order, where diverse nations are drawn together in common cause to achieve the universal aspirations of mankind—peace and security, freedom, and the rule of law. Such is a world worthy of our struggle, and worthy of our children's future."

"A new world order" based on a "common cause"! The drumbeat increases its cadence. Such concepts, foretold in Revelation 13, have become common currency throughout Europe and the United States!

Last act in the drama

A significant time factor kicks in at this point—the enforcement of Sunday laws worldwide becomes the "last act in the drama. When this substitution becomes universal, God will reveal himself. When the laws of men are exalted above the laws of God, when the powers of this earth try to force men to keep the first day of the week, know that the time has come for God to work."[24]

Obviously this is almost too much to contemplate at this time. Adventists are known the world over as law-abiding, law-supporting people. In addition, American Adventists are also known for their unambiguous defense of liberty, even willing to die for these freedoms when their president calls for their services in time of war.

But because of world panic and the crafty manipulation of legislators and jurists, "the whole world is to be stirred with enmity against Seventh-day Adventists."[25] And *pseudo-logic* will prevail: "The whole world keeps Sunday, they say, and why should not this people, who are so few in number, do according to the laws of the land?"[26]

"The judges will refuse to listen to the reasons of those who are loyal to the commandments of God, because they know that arguments in favor of the fourth commandment are unanswerable. They will say, 'We have a law, and by our law he ought to die.' God's law is nothing to them. 'Our law' with them is supreme. Those who respect this human law will be favored, but those who will not bow to the idol sabbath have no favors shown them."[27]

Adventists in many levels of government and in the academic and business world will discover that their friends of "wealth, genius, [and] education, will combine to cover them with contempt. Persecuting rulers, ministers, and church members will conspire against them. With voice and pen, by boasts, threats, and ridicule, they will seek to overthrow their faith. . . . [They] shall be treated as traitors."[28] "Those who honor the Bible Sabbath will be denounced as enemies of law and order, as breaking down the moral restraints of society, causing anarchy and corruption, and calling down the judgments of God upon the earth. Their conscientious scruples will be pronounced obstinacy, stubbornness, and contempt of authority."[29]

Word games

Of course, governments must balance liberty of the individual with security of the individual. The problem is that governments often play word games with these concepts, using phrases such as "antiterrorism," "child protection," and "common values" to attack the constitutional rights of a supposed enemy or opponent. Emotional identification with euphemistic words snared Germans under Hitler. Let's not believe such political manipulation could never happen again. In the name of freedom, well-intentioned prosecutors and courts can easily mask and override such fundamental rights as preventive detention, right to counsel, the right to prepare a defense, the right to interview and call witnesses, the right to trial and due process before sentencing. These are basic rights that tens of thousands of Americans have fought and died for.

If ever there was a time for mental and moral clarity in the Adventist Church, it is now! It is now time for Adventist lawyers and judges to speak out in defense of God-given individual freedoms when it comes to conscience and core beliefs. It is now time—before the storm breaks—for church leadership, pastors, and administrators to think boldly regarding their responsibility to guide the church to think carefully about these issues.

A powerful heads-up

Let's not think, complacently, that "these things will not happen in my day!" Let's not think that predicted defections from the church and its attending confusion will come from groups other than our own. Consider the following prediction—one that is as certain as the prediction that Jesus will return:

> As the storm approaches, a large class who have professed faith in the third angel's message, but have not been sanctified through obedience to the truth, abandon their position and

join the ranks of the opposition. By uniting with the world and partaking of its spirit, they have come to view matters in nearly the same light; and when the test is brought, they are prepared to choose the easy, popular side. Men of talent and pleasing address, who once rejoiced in the truth, employ their powers to deceive and mislead souls. They become the most bitter enemies of their former brethren. When Sabbathkeepers are brought before the courts to answer for their faith, these apostates are the most efficient agents of Satan to misrepresent and accuse them, and by false reports and insinuations to stir up the rulers against them.[30]

If this preview of things to come is not a powerful heads-up, then I don't know what can get our attention.

In the past forty years, Western society has seen a shift toward what sociologists are calling a postmodern period, in which the authority of objective truth is abandoned and personal feelings and opinions have become the basis for "truth." Ellen White highlights how this shift in thinking will play out in the closing days of earth:

As the claims of the fourth commandment are urged upon the people, it is found that the observance of the seventh-day Sabbath is enjoined, and as the only way to free themselves from a duty which they are unwilling to perform, many popular teachers declare that the law of God is no longer binding. Thus they cast away the law and the Sabbath together. As the work of Sabbath reform extends, this rejection of the divine law to avoid the claims of the fourth commandment will become well-nigh universal. The teachings of religious leaders have opened the door to infidelity, to spiritualism, and to contempt for God's holy law; and upon these leaders rests a fearful responsibility for the iniquity that exists in the Christian world.

Yet this very class put forth the claim that the fast-spreading corruption is largely attributable to the desecration of the so-called "Christian sabbath," and that the enforcement of Sunday observance would greatly improve the morals of society.[31]

After predicting end-time disasters of all kinds and that "these visitations are to become more and more frequent and disastrous," she wrote,

> Then the great deceiver will persuade men that those who serve God are causing these evils. The class that have provoked the displeasure of Heaven will charge all their troubles upon those whose obedience to God's commandments is a perpetual reproof to transgressors. It will be declared that men are offending God by the violation of the Sunday sabbath; that this sin has brought calamities which will not cease until Sunday observance shall be strictly enforced; and that those who present the claims of the fourth commandment, thus destroying reverence for Sunday, are troublers of the people, preventing their restoration to divine favor and temporal prosperity.[32]

Even more explicitly, Ellen White previewed how those proclaiming the legitimacy of the seventh day of the week as the biblical Sabbath would be declared "lawbreakers."[33]

> Those who honor the Bible Sabbath will be denounced as enemies of law and order, as breaking down the moral restraints of society, causing anarchy and corruption, and calling down the judgments of God upon the earth. Their conscientious scruples will be pronounced obstinacy, stubbornness, and contempt of authority. They will be accused of disaffection toward the government. Ministers who deny the obligation of the divine law will

present from the pulpit the duty of yielding obedience to the civil authorities as ordained of God. In legislative halls and courts of justice, commandment keepers will be misrepresented and condemned. A false coloring will be given to their words; the worst construction will be put upon their motives.[34]

Review of nineteenth-century predictions

In the nineteenth century, such unambiguous forecasts were only an outline of the future in the United States and the rest of the world. Today, in the beginning of the twenty-first century, we are living in a time of an enormous and spectacular unfolding of these predicted insights:

- Protestant spokesmen declare that God's law is no longer binding and that the seventh-day Sabbath was a Jewish custom—thus removing the religious argument for the authority of the fourth commandment of the Decalogue.
- At the same time, others will declare that calamities are the result of God's displeasure at the violation of the Sunday-sabbath.
- The rise of end-time corruption and regaining God's blessings and temporal prosperity become reasons for supporting Sunday sacredness.
- A colossal increase in the frequency and severity of natural disasters will become a further reason for national action regarding Sunday observance as a way of showing God the nation's collective repentance.
- When supporters of the seventh-day Sabbath continue their defense of religious liberty and the biblical Sabbath, they will be denounced as enemies of law and order.
- In the halls of justice, supporters of the biblical Sabbath will be misrepresented and condemned. A false coloring will be given to their defense of freedom and biblical authority.

National apostasy and national ruin

Mrs. White noted that when a Sunday law is enacted in the United States, "national apostasy will be followed by national ruin."[35] "National ruin" could take various forms, but it will clearly be something significant that will affect everyone—perhaps something akin to the collapse of the stock market and the national economy. Whatever is involved, it will add to the desperation of a nation that is looking for scapegoats.[36]

The Sunday law phenomenon will not be limited to the United States or even to Western civilization: "As America, the land of religious liberty, shall unite with the papacy in forcing the conscience and compelling men to honor the false sabbath, the people of every country on the globe will be led to follow her example."[37]

These two predictions are ominous. This linkage is probably the only detail in the saga of the United States in prophecy that is still on the horizon. When I think of "national apostasy," I am reminded of another Ellen White observation: "There are not many, even among educators and statesmen, who comprehend the causes that underlie the present state of society. Those who hold the reins of government are not able to solve the problem of moral corruption, poverty, pauperism, and increasing crime. They are struggling in vain to place business operations on a more secure basis."[38]

"National apostasy" will prompt further the national urge for a unity of people sharing common values. It also parallels the ripening of earth's harvest—the ripening of the wheat and the tares, a sure sign of Christ's return (Revelation 14:14–16).

No one today can accurately imagine how all this will play out. We can only guess at the national crises that will generate a call for national unity of those who will vote for common values in the hope that God can bring peace to the nation. All the while, this surge for national unity leading to Sunday enforcement will bring out the worst in people who prefer legislation rather than dialogue over the issues that divide.

The various crises will feed on each other, whether they be economic collapse, terrorism, rampant disease, or natural disasters. The result will be "national ruin" and the prelude to the seven last plagues. Probation will close. The neural pathways of faithful loyalists who regard the commandments of God as their hedge and joy are settled into the truth so that they will never, ever, say No to God. The neural pathways of those who have rejected the wooing of the Holy Spirit are also settled into a pattern of self-will and absorption. They too will never change—habit patterns are set forever.

Specific counsel to God's loyalists

Does Ellen White have anything specific to say regarding those who remain loyal to God's commandments? Much in many ways:

- "Every earthly support" will be "cut off."[39]
- "Hoarded wealth will soon be worthless."[40]
- "Some . . . will be thrust into prison."[41]
- "Friends will prove treacherous, and will betray us. Relatives, deceived by the enemy, will think they do God service . . . , hoping we will deny our faith."[42]
- "When the defiance of the law of Jehovah shall be almost universal, when His people shall be pressed in affliction by their fellow men, God will interpose."[43]
- "The people of God will not be free from suffering [after the close of probation]; but while persecuted and distressed, while they endure privation and suffer for want of food, they will not be left to perish."[44]
- "In the time of trouble just before the coming of Christ, the righteous will be preserved through the ministration of heavenly angels."[45]

What should we conclude?

What may have seemed far-fetched in the middle of the nineteenth century is front-page news today. Although the world influence of the papacy and the United States was many years in the future, biblical scholars such as John N. Andrews painted an amazing scenario of what was to come, on the basis of Bible study alone. Ellen White emphatically enlarged this biblical picture in ways that no one on earth could have imagined in her day. But how precisely her predictions have become daily reality!

Adventists don't get their prophetic understanding from reading today's news. They never have and never will. They let the newsmakers validate the prophetic road map, not write it. In other words, they don't re-create their view of last-day events in every new generation. They "have the prophetic word made more sure" (2 Peter 1:19).

Adventists in the nineteenth century may have had to use their imaginations. Adventists today have only to use their eyes and ears. Nightfall does not come at once. At twilight, everything remains seemingly unchanged. But at twilight we should sense the coolness of the air, lest we suddenly become victims of the darkness.

God never leaves His people without "present truth"

Why did God give this picture of the future to Ellen White? Because He has never left His people without "present truth." John the revelator wrote that in the end time, the papacy's "deadly wound was healed" (Revelation 13:12). That time has come—much beyond anyone's anticipation even forty years ago!

God has never stood by, merely watching His loyalists face up to tough times. In the past, He has always given them the guidance they need to follow His leading, and He will do so again in the future. "Surely the Lord God does nothing, / Unless He reveals His secret to His servants the prophets" (Amos 3:7).

Furthermore, and just as important, Jesus knows what men and women need in times of great stress *because He has been here*. He knows by personal experience that only a firm grasp of truth can prepare a person to withstand Satan's fiercest temptations. People in the end time will face a crisis, "a time of trouble, such as never was since there was a nation" (Daniel 12:1). Jesus knows firsthand what those fierce temptations can be!

Ellen White offers end-time people clear, believable counsel: "In order to endure the trial before them, they must understand the will of God as revealed in his Word; they can honor him only as they have a right conception of His character, government, and purposes, and act in accordance with them. None but those who have fortified the mind with the truths of the Bible will stand through the last great conflict."[46]

Our response to God's graciousness and the counsel of His last-day messenger is to keep walking into the light until the Light Bearer returns. Everyone in the world has enough light to make moral decisions, even though it may be only the light shining through a very small crack in the door.

No other people have a clearer map for the road ahead. No other people have been given the responsibility of sharing the truth about the future with others. How will we ever face up to reality when we realize that we knew something about the future that we could have made clearer to our children, to our neighbors, to men and women everywhere—but we neglected this privilege and duty?

The only peaceful, reassuring way to face the last of the last days is to keep trusting God's Word, which alone can give us the road map.

---

1. See LeRoy E. Froom, *The Prophetic Faith of Our Fathers* (Washington, D.C.: Review and Herald® Publishing Association, 1948), 4:1091–1103.

2. Ibid., 1099, 1104.

3. E. G. White, *The Great Controversy* (1888 ed.), 579.

4. E. G. White, *Testimonies for the Church*, 5:451 (1885) (see chap. 1, n. 5).

5. E. G. White, *The Great Controversy*, 445 (see chap. 2, n. 10).

6. Ibid., 588.

7. Ibid., 578, 579.

8. Ibid., 592.

9. Ellen G. White, *Review and Herald*, December 18, 1888.

10. Ellen G. White, *Review and Herald*, May 2, 1893.

11. E. G. White, *Testimonies for the Church*, 6:18.

12. Ibid., 395.

13. By executive order on December 12, 2002, President Bush launched his Faith-Based Initiative, a program that promotes federal funding of faith-based organizations. Although, funding has been available to religious social service agencies for many years, this executive order permits direct federal funding to churches. Gerald C. Grimaud, former Pennsylvania assistant attorney general and currently in private practice in Tunkhannock, Pennsylvania, wrote, "With the breakdown of the wall of separation, both church and state will pay a great price, as will the individual. Yes, church social programs and the needy will benefit in the short run. However, with state funding comes government intrusion into church programs; forms, applications, questions, monitoring, supervising, auditing, regulating, managing, and even prosecutions. And over time, sadly, the mission of church programs will be neutered." "Breakdown of the Wall," *Liberty*, March/April 2003.

14. *Korematsu v. United States*, 1943.

15. Alexis de Tocqueville, *Democracy in America* (New York, N.Y.: Signet Classic, 2001), 120.

16. Samuele Bacchiocchi, "Endtime Issues," no. 100, June 22, 2003.

17. Web site for the Ten Commandment Commission: http://tencommandmentsday.com/home.html.

18. Pat Robertson, *The New World Order* (Dallas: Word Publishing, 1991), 233.

19. Ibid., 236.

20. See the previous chapter for more elaboration of this apostolic letter: "62. It is the duty of Christians therefore to remember that, although the practices of the Jewish Sabbath are gone, surpassed as they are by the 'fulfillment' which Sunday brings, the underlying reasons for keeping 'the Lord's Day' holy—inscribed solemnly in the Ten Commandments—remain valid, though they need to be reinterpreted in the light of the theology and spirituality of Sunday. . . . 64. For several centuries, Christians observed Sunday simply as a day of worship, without being able to give it the specific meaning of Sabbath rest. Only in the fourth century did the civil law of the Roman Empire recognize the weekly recurrence, determining that on 'the day of the sun' the judges, the people of the cities and the various trade corporations would not work. . . . 65. By contrast, the link between the Lord's Day and the day of rest in civil society has a meaning and importance, which go beyond the distinctly

Christian point of view. The alternation between work and rest, built into human nature, is willed by God himself, as appears in the creation story in the Book of Genesis. . . . In this matter, my predecessor Pope Leo XIII in his Encyclical *Rerum Novarum* speaks of Sunday rest as a worker's right which the State must guarantee. In our own historical context there remains the obligations to ensure that everyone can enjoy the freedom, rest and relaxation which human dignity requires, together with the associated religious, family, cultural and interpersonal needs which are difficult to meet if there is no guarantee of at least one day of the week on which people can *both* rest and celebrate. . . . 67. . . . Therefore, also in the particular circumstances of our own time, Christians will naturally strive to ensure that civil legislation respects their duty to keep Sunday holy."—*"Dies Domini,"* July 7, 1998.

21. Ellen G. White, *Last Day Events* (Nampa, Idaho: Pacific Press® Publishing Association, 1992), 135.

22. Ibid.

23. Jay Tolson, "The New American Empire?" *U.S. News & World Report*, January 13, 2003.

24. *Review and Herald*, April 23, 1901.

25. E. G. White, *Last Day Events*, 136.

26. Ibid.

27. Ellen G. White, *Signs of the Times*, May 26, 1898.

28. E. G. White, *Last Day Events*, 146.

29. E. G. White, *The Great Controversy*, 592.

30. Ibid., 608.

31. Ibid., 587.

32. Ibid., 590.

33. Ibid., 591.

34. Ibid., 592.

35. E. G. White, *Review and Herald,* December 18, 1888. Ellen G. White Comments, *Seventh-day Adventist Bible Commentary*, vol. 7, 977 (see chap. 5, n. 15).

36. See E. G. White, *Selected Messages*, vol. 2, 373 (see chap. 2, n. 3).

37. E. G. White, *Testimonies for the Church*, 6:18.

38. Ibid., 9:13.

39. E. G. White, *The Desire of Ages*, 121, 122 (see chap. 4, n. 33).

40. *Review and Herald*, March 21, 1878.

41. E. G. White, *The Great Controversy*, 608.

42. E. G. White, *Maranatha* (Washington, D.C.: Review and Herald® Publishing Association, 1976), 197.

43. *Review and Herald*, June 15, 1897.

44. E. G. White, *The Great Controversy*, 629.

45. E. G. White, *Patriarchs and Prophets* (Mountain View, Calif.: Pacific Press® Publishing Association, 1958), 256.

46. E. G. White, *The Great Controversy*, 593, 594.

Chapter Seven

ELLEN WHITE'S SUPREME CONTRIBUTION—THE GREAT CONTROVERSY VISIONS

Without question, Ellen White's most significant contribution grew out of the broad strokes of her first vision, given in December 1844. This vision was amplified more precisely in 1858 and in many subsequent visions. Referred to as "the great controversy theme," the scope and implication of these visions became the intellectual steel girders for all her writings, including such areas as education, mental and physical health, theology, and business. Her great controversy theme made each of these areas not only distinctive but also highly interrelated.

The great controversy theme spells out the cause of sin and why God chose not to destroy Lucifer. Rather than destroy the creator of evil, God permitted the awful consequences of rebellion to play out so that the whole universe could see the self-defeating principles that Lucifer-turned-Satan had held up as the better way to run the universe.

After this world became involved with Adam and Eve's fateful choices in Eden, God immediately began to tell His side of the story in the hopes of winning the loyalty of earth's inhabitants. The core principles of that story would reflect the way that God's loyalists should think and act.

Ellen White summarized the basic element in God's rescue plan in these words: "The grand central thought . . . the central theme of the Bible, the theme about which every other in the whole book clusters, is the redemption plan, the restoration in the human soul of the image of God."[1]

In other words, God's goal in the great controversy is to undo sin's damage and to restore His image in men and women as reflected in the life and character of Jesus. In Him, we learn that Satan—not God—is the destroyer. God is light and not darkness; He is our Restorer. *And, the goal of the gospel is our restoration, not only our forgiveness.*

Reflecting this biblical message, Ellen wrote, "The religion of Christ means more than the forgiveness of sin; it means taking away our sins, and filling the vacuum with the graces of the Holy Spirit. . . . The glory, the fullness, the completeness of the gospel plan is fulfilled in the life."[2]

Clarifying our terms

What do we mean when we use the phrase *the great controversy?* Some think of the controversy being waged between good and evil, light and darkness. Some think of the controversy between God and the heathen nations (see Jeremiah 25:31). Some instantly think of the title of the fifth volume in the series of books known as the Conflict of the Ages, written by Ellen White. But Ellen White uses the phrase *the great controversy* to describe the biblical controversy between God and Satan, from its beginning in heaven to its conclusion in the earth made new. That understanding is what we will now trace in her various visions. Let's track Ellen White's developing understanding of God's rescue plan as He restores in forgiven rebels all that sin has damaged.

The first vision

In her December 1844 vision, the first of about two thousand that would follow, Ellen White "saw" a path leading from the disappointment of 1844 to the City of God. A light from behind, shining on the path, depicted the validity of the 1844 experience and gave those traveling the path confidence that they were on a safe journey. A light ahead encouraged them even though the path to the City would require perseverance and commitment. Some would leave the path as they fell back into worldly pleasures. So for the travelers looking forward toward the bright light of the Advent hope, the struggles foreseen would be worth the commitment.[3]

Four years later, the grand sweep of the controversy was again presented to Ellen White, but she gave scant reference to it in written form except for the limited description in her first book, *A Sketch of the Christian Experiences and Views of Ellen G. White* (1851).

The vision known today as "the great controversy vision"

On the weekend of March 13 and 14, 1858, James and Ellen White were attending meetings in Lovett's Grove, Ohio. On Sunday, March 14, James conducted a funeral service. After his sermon, Ellen, now thirty years of age, arose to say comforting words to the mourners. Soon she was in vision. For about two hours her audience remained, observing the remarkable event. Later she wrote, "In the vision at Lovett's Grove, most of the matter which I had seen ten years before [1848] concerning the great controversy of the ages between Christ and Satan, was repeated, and I was instructed to write it out. I was shown that while I should have to contend with the powers of darkness, for Satan would make strong efforts to hinder me, yet I must put my trust in God, and angels would not leave me in the conflict."[4]

On the train ride home, James and Ellen White decided that Ellen's first task should be to write out the vision and prepare it for publication. Little did they realize the significance of the Lord's warning regarding Satan's "strong efforts to hinder" her.

Stopping at Jackson, Michigan, to visit their old friends Mr. and Mrs. Daniel Palmer, early converts of Joseph Bates, young Ellen was afflicted with paralysis: "As I was conversing with Sister Palmer, my tongue refused to utter what I wished to say, and seemed large and numb. A strange, cold sensation struck my heart, passed over my head, and down my right side. For a time I was insensible, but was aroused by the voice of earnest prayer. I tried to use my left limbs, but they were perfectly useless."[5]

The next day, after her strength was partially restored, the Whites returned home to Battle Creek, Michigan. Though suffering intensely, Ellen began to write out the weekend's vision. Later, she recalled: "At first I could write but one page a day, and then rest three days; but as I progressed, my strength increased. The numbness in my head did not seem to becloud my mind, and before I closed that work [*Spiritual Gifts*, volume 1] the effect of the shock had entirely left me."[6]

Satan's sudden attack

In June 1858, while completing this first written record of her great controversy vision, Ellen received another vision that provided further background to her experience in the Palmer home, three months earlier: "I was shown in vision that in the sudden attack at Jackson, Satan intended to take my life, in order to hinder the work I was about to write; but angels of God were sent to my rescue."[7]

The 219 pages of *Spiritual Gifts*, volume 1, published in September 1858, contained three brief chapters devoted to "The Fall of Satan," the "Fall of Man," and "The Plan of Salvation." Passing over events in the Old Testament, thirteen chapters covered the life and ministry of Jesus and the apostles. The remaining chapters dealt with the great apostasy through the Reformation, and then recounted earth's closing events, ending with the second death. (After several printings, a new edition of *Spiritual Gifts*, volume 1, was published in 1882 as a single volume; later in the same year, *Spiritual Gifts*, volume 1, also became the last section of the new book, *Early Writings*.) After the publication of *Spiritual Gifts*, volume 1, Ellen White returned to completing an autobiographical work that was published in 1860 as *Spiritual Gifts*, volume 2, containing 304 pages.

But overriding all else, Ellen White stayed focused on the great controversy. The panoramic vision of 1858 was to be more fully written out. In 1864, *Spiritual Gifts*, volumes 3 and 4 were published, dealing more comprehensively with the fall of Satan, the Creation, the fall of Adam and Eve, the lives of the patriarchs, and later Jewish history.

Update needed

As the years passed and membership of the Adventist movement increased in numbers, a new printing of *Spiritual Gifts*, volumes 1–4 was needed. But Mrs. White wanted no more reprints until she had time to greatly update these books with the revelations she had received in the interim. The result was a four-volume set of books, each about four hundred pages, under the general title of *Spirit of Prophecy*, volumes 1–4. Volume 1 was completed in 1870; volume 2, in 1877; volume 3, in 1878; and volume 4, in 1884. Volume 4 was especially constructed to outline the great controversy as it developed in the first century of the Christian era and through the Reformation period so that people in modern times could understand more clearly the issues involved. (Generally speaking, this was the first edition of the book that we know today as *The Great Controversy*.)

In the early 1880s, church leaders began to see the possibility of making Adventist doctrines available to the general public through door-to-door contacts. They saw how chapters from *Spiritual Gifts*, volumes 1–4 were being received when printed in the church's missionary paper, *Signs of the Times*. Publishers also observed how readily the general public welcomed Uriah Smith's book *Daniel and the Revelation*. Thus, between 1885 and 1888, ten printings of volume 4 were produced on heavier paper, with wider margins and twenty-two full-page illustrations—the first Ellen White book to carry illustrations.

More amplification during European trip

But the story of the great controversy visions moves on. From 1885 to 1887 Ellen White was in Europe. Visits to many of the Reformation cities, especially specific historic sites, brought her flashbacks of previous visions that had been described in *Spiritual Gifts*, volume 4. These helped her to write even more graphically about such events as the persecution of the Waldenses in Torre Pellice and Zwingli's Zurich. Translations of *Spiritual Gifts*, especially volume 4, into the major European languages contained additions that were carried into the English-language *Conflict of the Ages* series, which Ellen White was already working on while in Europe.

This continuing unfolding of the cosmic controversy between Christ and Satan increased in intensity while she was in Europe. As she rewrote and amplified the whole great controversy story, Ellen White recognized that some of the phrases and expressions in *Spiritual Gifts*, volumes 1–4 would be immediately understood by Adventists but not by the general public. This resulted in certain changes. For instance, the first four pages of the chapter "The Snares of Satan" were omitted from the 1888 edition of *The Great Controversy*, the fifth book in the *Conflict of the Ages* series. Why? Because they dealt with how Satan would eventually use Protestant ministers against Seventh-day Sabbath keepers in the end time—and the general public would not have the background to understand this point. (In 1923, these deleted pages were reprinted in *Testimonies to Ministers*, pages 472–474, a book printed for an Adventist audience.)

The 1888 edition of the *Spirit of Prophecy*, volume 4—labeled "Revised and Enlarged" and now titled *The Great Controversy*—had 678 pages instead of the 492 pages of the 1884 book it was replacing. This new edition contained twenty-six full-page illustrations, and the appendix was expanded.[8]

Remarkable introduction

But the most important feature of this latest unfolding of the great controversy story is the remarkable preface, later called the introduction, for the 1888 book. Ellen White wrote it herself; this was the only book for which she wrote her own introduction. Personally, I have found these eight pages to be the most helpful description I have ever read of how God worked with and through his prophets. In the clearest language possible, without the ambiguity that one usually finds in the attempts of others to analyze how revelation and inspiration work, Ellen White explains why biblical writers, often writing on the same subject or event, differ in details and in insight.

If those who have raised questions regarding Ellen White's authenticity and reliability—or who have believed unfair charges against her integrity as God's messenger—had taken the time to read and understand her own introduction explaining the process of inspiration, I believe their questions and charges would have melted away as Jell-O in the July sun.

Use of borrowed material

In this introduction to the 1888 edition of *The Great Controversy*, Ellen White carefully described how and why she used various sources in the development of her books. She employed the same principle that Bible writers used when borrowing the material of uninspired authors: To speed truth along, inspired writers, at times, utilized borrowed expressions that would better clothe their thoughts with precision and the force of beauty. For Ellen White's readers, such usage was no problem—if they kept their eyes on the big picture of the core message. The big picture of the great controversy theme was the determining issue for Ellen White, not the borrowing that added beauty and precision of thought to the big picture.

Mrs. White was transparent in the use of borrowed material:

In some cases where a historian has so grouped together events as to afford, in brief, a comprehensive view of the subject, or has summarized details in a convenient manner, his words have been quoted; but in some instances no specific credit has been given, since the quotations are not given for the purpose of citing that writer as authority, but because his statement affords a ready and forcible presentation of the subject. In narrating the experience and views of those carrying on the work of reform in our own time, similar use has been made of their published works.[9]

Some may question the inspirational value of borrowed material, but it seems logical that if God revealed His message to His prophets, He would also assist them in conveying that message in human language, making the best use of whatever could enhance that message. Ellen White noted, in her introduction, that God "guided the mind in the selection of what to speak and what to write. The treasure was entrusted to earthen vessels, yet it is, nonetheless, from Heaven."[10] In other words, the prophet was in charge of whether the borrowed material would enhance the message or not.

The pagination of the 1888 edition of *The Great Controversy* became the standard for the revised edition that appeared in 1911.

End-time truths highlighted in *The Great Controversy* volume

Each of the five volumes in the Conflict set highlights key aspects of the great controversy theme. But this volume, the fifth in the Conflict series, underlines Ellen White's golden thread of the cosmic controversy. Note these key points:

1. Probation will close at a time when the world will be basking in a sense of optimism and hope of progress to come.

Come when it may, the day of God will come unawares to the ungodly. When life is going on in its unvarying round; when men are absorbed in pleasure, in business, in traffic, in money-making; when religious leaders are magnifying the world's progress and enlightenment, and the people are lulled in a false security—then, as the midnight thief steals within the unguarded dwelling, so shall sudden destruction come upon the careless and ungodly, "and they shall not escape." 1 Thessalonians 5:3.[11]

2. Two basic classes would develop in the Christian church— those who see faith as a life change in response to our Lord's gifts of forgiveness and cleansing, and those who see faith as only a mental acceptance of what Jesus did on the Cross.

Satan therefore laid his plans to war more successfully against the government of God by planting his banner in the Christian church. . . .

The great adversary now endeavored to gain by artifice what he had failed to secure by force. . . . Idolaters were led to receive a part of the Christian faith, while they rejected other essential truths. They professed to accept Jesus as the Son of God and to believe in His death and resurrection, but they had no conviction of sin and felt no need of repentance or of a change of heart. With some concessions on their part they proposed that Christians should make concessions, that all might unite on the platform of belief in Christ.[12]

3. Satan would enlist the aid of the Christian church in further-ing his lies about the character of God.

The teachings of popes and priests had led men to look

upon the character of God, and even of Christ, as stern, gloomy, and forbidding. The Saviour was represented as so far devoid of sympathy with man in his fallen state that the mediation of priests and saints must be invoked. Those whose minds had been enlightened by the word of God longed to point these souls to Jesus as their compassionate, loving Saviour, standing with outstretched arms, inviting all to come to Him with their burden of sin, their care and weariness. They longed to clear away the obstructions which Satan had piled up that men might not see the promises, and come directly to God, confessing their sins, and obtaining pardon and peace.[13]

4. John Wesley recognized that justification and sanctification are joined—clearly teaching that we can't have one without the other.

Wesley's life was devoted to the preaching of the great truths which he had received—justification through faith in the atoning blood of Christ, and the renewing power of the Holy Spirit upon the heart, bringing forth fruit in a life conformed to the example of Christ.[14]

5. Men and women have significant responsibility in the salvation process.

Through the grace of God and their own diligent effort they must be conquerors in the battle with evil. While the investigative judgment is going forward in heaven, while the sins of penitent believers are being removed from the sanctuary, there is to be a special work of purification, of putting away of sin, among God's people upon earth.[15]

6. In his assaults on Christians, one of Satan's prime strategies is to separate Christ's life and death from His high-priestly ministry.

The archdeceiver hates the great truths that bring to view an atoning sacrifice and an all-powerful mediator. He knows that with him everything depends on his diverting minds from Jesus and His truth.[16]

7. Satan hates the profound linkage between Christ's work on the Cross and His work as our High Priest and seeks to separate the two concepts in the minds of Christians because he knows that if he can succeed in doing so, we will not have both the desire and the ability to overcome sin.

The subject of the sanctuary and the investigative judgment should be clearly understood by the people of God. All need knowledge for themselves of the position and work of their great High Priest. Otherwise it will be impossible for them to exercise the faith which is essential at this time or to occupy the position which God designs them to fill. . . .

The intercession of Christ in man's behalf in the sanctuary above is as essential to the plan of salvation as was His death upon the cross. By His death He began that work which after His resurrection He ascended to complete in heaven. . . .

. . . If those who hide and excuse their faults could see how Satan exults over them, how he taunts Christ and holy angels with their course, they would make haste to confess their sins and to put them away. Through defects in the character, Satan works to gain control of the whole mind, and he knows that if these defects are cherished, he will succeed. Therefore he is constantly seeking to deceive the followers of Christ with his fatal sophistry that it is impossible for them to overcome.[17]

8. The universe will know when the great controversy is over and everything that God has said from the beginning has been vindicated. And never again will there be an occasion for any created being to distrust God.

> The whole universe will have become witnesses to the nature and results of sin. And its utter extermination, which in the beginning would have brought fear to angels and dishonor to God, will now vindicate His love and establish His honor before the universe of beings who delight to do His will, and in whose heart is His law. Never will evil again be manifest. Says the word of God: "Affliction shall not rise up the second time." Nahum 1:9. The law of God, which Satan has reproached as the yoke of bondage, will be honored as the law of liberty. A tested and proved creation will never again be turned from allegiance to Him whose character has been fully manifested before them as fathomless love and infinite wisdom.[18]

Great controversy theme amplified throughout the "Conflicts"

With the 1888 edition of *The Great Controversy* now available, Ellen White turned to enlarging the first volume in The Spirit of Prophecy series. We know this book today as the 714-page *Patriarchs and Prophets*, completed in 1890.

She ended this volume with the chapter "The Last Years of David," leaving the story of Solomon and all later Old Testament events for a new book that we now know as *Prophets and Kings*, but its publication had to wait until shortly after Ellen White's death.

In the development of the great controversy story, the first volume, *Patriarchs and Prophets*, stands shoulder to shoulder in importance with the fifth and last volume, now known as *The Great Controversy*—two sturdy bookends to the greatest story ever told. To be more specific, the great controversy story hinges on *Patriarchs and Prophets'* stunning unfolding of how sin began, why it was permitted to exist, and how it eventually will be eliminated from the universe. The next four volumes of the Conflict of the Ages set would be *virtually meaningless* without the dramatic background given in the first volume describing how God chose to deal with the sin problem.

In *Patriarchs and Prophets* many core principles in the great controversy were chiseled into eternal granite. These examples are significant:

1. The highest purpose of the controversy is to vindicate God's character that Satan has sorely misrepresented—not the salvation of men and women on planet earth.

   But the plan of redemption had a yet broader and deeper purpose than the salvation of man. It was not for this alone that Christ came to the earth; it was not merely that the inhabitants of this little world might regard the law of God as it should be regarded; but it was to vindicate the character of God before the universe.[19]

2. Satan had accused God of being unjust and that He arbitrarily made laws that were faulty; Satan argued that for the good of the universe these laws needed to be adjusted.

   From the first the great controversy had been upon the law of God. Satan had sought to prove that God was unjust, that His law was faulty, and that the good of the universe required it to be changed. In attacking the law he aimed to overthrow the authority of its Author. In the controversy it was to be shown whether the divine statutes were defective and subject to change, or perfect and immutable.[20]

Writing *The Desire of Ages*

For years, Ellen White had been writing on the life of Jesus. But as time went on, she realized that her periodical articles and her treatment of our Lord's life in volumes 2 and 3 of The Spirit of Prophecy were not adequate. This burden to further deal with Jesus' life throbbed through her many letters written after *Patriarchs and Prophets* had been completed.

Then something happened that Mrs. White had not foreseen—church leadership asked her to leave the United States and help pioneer the Adventist presence in Australia. Reluctantly at first, she left for this land on the other side of the world. Today, summing up the nine years she devoted to Australia, we can see that without Ellen White, the Adventist advance in the South Pacific would have been greatly retarded. Her admonitions, in person or in letters, launched a school system that needed her insights, energy, and financial support (she had to plead with friends around the world to *loan* her money to meet the needs).

However, during many of those arduous years, 1891–1900, she was in constant pain, afflicted with inflammatory rheumatism. For eleven months she was bedridden. When not in bed, she sat in a chair that had been fitted with adjustable supports to relieve her aching writing arm. Her time was filled with active correspondence with leaders in the United States as well as those in Australia—voluminous correspondence!

Finally in 1895, she knew that something had to change: "I have about decided to . . . devote all my time to writing for the books that ought to be prepared without further delay. I would like to write on the life of Christ, on Christian Temperance [*The Ministry of Healing*] and prepare testimony Number 34 [volume 6]. . . . You know that my whole theme both in the pulpit and in private, by voice and pen, is the life of Christ."[21]

Many find it interesting to learn that Mrs. White did not write *The Desire of Ages* continuously, starting with the first chapter and continuing through the eighty-seven chapters in order. As we have noted already, she had been writing on the life of Jesus for years. Many periodical articles, manuscripts, and letters, as well as her published books, became a gold mine from which she and her closest assistants gathered material for this new volume. After the material had been organized into the order Mrs. White wanted, she would add connective insights as she smoothed out the story, relating it in the words of charm and power that millions the world over have found so powerfully compelling.

But the gathered material was far too much for a single book. Wise decisions were made, and today we have, in addition to *The Desire of Ages*, the incomparable books known as *Thoughts From the Mount of Blessing* (1896), *Christ's Object Lessons* (1900), and parts of *The Ministry of Healing* (1905).

The Desire of Ages continued the grand panorama of the great controversy story—as we would expect. In clear language, Ellen White sets forth the reasons why a member of the Godhead became Jesus, humankind's Savior. Much of this biblical overview had been muted or lost in the two thousand years since His birth on this rebel planet. Here are some of the key thoughts she presents in this precious book:

1. Jesus became a baby as all babies did two thousand years ago, subject to the same laws of heredity, in order to show the universe that God's laws can be willingly kept, even by the descendants of Adam and Eve.

We marvel at the Saviour's sacrifice in exchanging the throne of heaven for the manger, and the companionship of adoring angels for the beasts of the stall. Human pride and self-sufficiency stand rebuked in His presence. Yet this was but the beginning of His wonderful condescension. It would have been an almost infinite humiliation for the Son of God to take man's nature, even when Adam stood in his innocence in Eden. But Jesus accepted humanity when the race had been weakened by four thousand years of sin. Like every child of Adam He accepted the results of the working of the great law of heredity. What these results were is shown in the history of His earthly ancestors. He came with such a heredity to share our sorrows and temptations, and to give us the example of a sinless life.

Satan in heaven had hated Christ for His position in the courts of God. He hated Him the more when he himself was dethroned. He hated Him who pledged Himself to redeem a race of sinners. Yet into the world where Satan claimed dominion God permitted His Son to come, a helpless babe, subject to the weakness of humanity. He permitted Him to meet life's peril in common with every human soul, to fight the battle as every child of humanity must fight it, at the risk of failure and eternal loss.[22]

2. Jesus became a human being such as we are so that we could have the assurance that we, too, can be overcomers as He was.

Satan represents God's law of love as a law of selfishness. He declares that it is impossible for us to obey its precepts. The fall of our first parents, with all the woe that has resulted, he charges upon the Creator, leading men to look upon God as the author of sin, and suffering, and death. Jesus was to unveil this deception. As one of us He was to give an example of obedience. For this He took upon Himself our nature, and passed through our experiences. "In all things it behooved Him to be made like unto His brethren." Heb. 2:17. If we had to bear anything which Jesus did not endure, then upon this point Satan would represent the power of God as insufficient for us. Therefore Jesus was "in all points tempted like as we are." Heb. 4:15. He endured every trial to which we are subject. And He exercised in His own behalf no power that is not freely offered to us. As man, He met temptation, and overcame in the strength given Him from God. He says, "I delight to do Thy will, O My God: yea, Thy law is within My heart." Ps. 40:8. As He went about doing good, and healing all who were afflicted by Satan, He made plain to men the character of God's law and the nature of His service. His life testifies that it is possible for us also to obey the law of God.[23]

3. The primary work of the Holy Spirit is to help former rebels become God's trusted loyalists—a work as important in the plan of salvation as was Christ's life and death.

The Spirit was to be given as a regenerating agent, and without this the sacrifice of Christ would have been of no avail. The power of evil had been strengthening for centuries, and the submission of men to this satanic captivity was amazing. Sin could be resisted and overcome only through the mighty agency of the Third Person of the Godhead, who would come with no modified energy, but in the fullness of divine power. It is the Spirit that makes effectual what has been wrought out by the world's Redeemer. It is by the Spirit that the heart is made pure. Through the Spirit the believer becomes a partaker of the divine nature. Christ has given His

Spirit as a divine power to overcome all hereditary and culti-
vated tendencies to evil, and to impress His own character
upon His church.[24]

4. Men and women are to become an integral part of God's answer to Satan's charges in settling the great controversy.

Of the Spirit Jesus said, "He shall glorify Me." The Saviour
came to glorify the Father by the demonstration of His love;
so the Spirit was to glorify Christ by revealing His grace to
the world. The very image of God is to be reproduced in humanity. The honor of God, the honor of Christ, is involved in
the perfection of the character of His people.[25]

5. Satan's nefarious program will continue until the universe has
seen the consequences of rebellion.

It was God's purpose to place things on an eternal basis
of security, and in the councils of heaven it was decided that
time must be given for Satan to develop the principles which
were the foundation of his system of government. He had
claimed that these were superior to God's principles. Time
was given for the working of Satan's principles, that they
might be seen by the heavenly universe.[26]

Yet Satan was not then destroyed [at the Cross]. The angels did not even then understand all that was involved in
the great controversy. The principles at stake were to be
more fully revealed. And for the sake of man, Satan's existence must be continued. Man as well as angels must see
the contrast between the Prince of light and the prince of
darkness. He must choose whom he will serve.[27]

Completing the Conflict set

Although the pivotal moments in the great controversy story had been covered in *Patriarchs and Prophets*, *The Desire of Ages*, and *The Great Controversy*, much still remained to be covered in the biblical overview. One of those periods was the Old Testament story from the reign of Solomon to the birth of Jesus. Another was the New Testament story of the young Christian church during the first century after Christ's ascension to heaven.

And so the work began on these remaining books; Ellen White and her staff worked in the same way as they had in the preparation of *The Desire of Ages*. All of Ellen White's written works were combed and selections arranged first into what we now call *The Acts of the Apostles* (1911). She commented on this project:

> My work on the book *The Acts of the Apostles* is completed. In a few weeks you shall have a copy. I have had excellent help in preparing this work for the press. There are other writings that I desire to get before our people, that they may speak when my voice is silent. The book on Old Testament History [*Prophets and Kings*], which we hope to bring out next, will call for earnest effort. I am grateful for the help the Lord is giving me in the labors of faithful, trained workers, and that these workers are ready to carry forward this work as fast as it is possible.[28]

Throughout this period, Mrs. White was often asked to speak at camp meetings and general leadership meetings. How she blended her heavy correspondence, public messages, and writing on the Conflict volumes continues to amaze me!

But this remarkable life of writing and speaking suddenly stopped with her unfortunate fall in February 1915 and her death in July of the same year. When she died, Ellen White had completed all but two of the chapters planned for *Prophets and Kings*. But her faithful staff had her previous material on the remaining subjects, and they followed through in completing the project. The book was published in 1917.

Why the 1911 revision of *The Great Controversy* was needed

By 1907, the 1888 edition of *The Great Controversy* had been printed many times at publishing houses in Mountain View, California; Washington, D.C.; and Watford, England; the printing plates were badly worn. Individual printing plates were reset as they wore out and were integrated into the existing plates, but the publishing houses were reluctant to reset the whole book for financial reasons.

On July 25, 1911, Ellen White wrote,

> When I learned that *Great Controversy* must be reset, I determined that we would have everything closely examined, to see if the truths it contained were stated in the very best manner, to convince those not of our faith that the Lord had guided and sustained me in the writing of its pages.
>
> As a result of the thorough examination by our most experienced workers, some changing in the wording has been proposed. These changes I have carefully examined, and approved. I am thankful that my life has been spared, and that I have strength and clearness of mind for this and other literary work.[29]

Obviously, a revision of such a revered book would raise questions, *especially from those who had not taken the time to read Mrs. White's own introduction to the book*. And especially from those who believed in verbal inspiration, that every word of a prophet's message was dictated by God. "Major revisions included an enlargement of the index from twelve to twenty-two pages; many more historical references added; stylistic changes bringing the revision into harmony with *Patriarchs and Prophets* and *The Desire of Ages*; several forms of expression were changed to avoid unnecessary offense such as 'Romish' to 'Roman.' "[30]

In summary, the revision, from start to finish, was done entirely within Ellen White's office and under her supervision; the changes that were made were changes that she said were "carefully examined, and approved."

Conclusion

Ellen White's unfolding of the great controversy story became the permeating theme in all of her writing for seventy years. That theme not only presented God's side of the controversy but also encompassed the response that men and women should make to God's plan for their salvation. Biblical terms such as *grace, faith, righteousness by faith,* etc., had been dreadfully misunderstood through the centuries by both Roman Catholics and most Protestants.

Ellen White's distinctive contribution has been to revisit these biblical terms, recovering their basic, unalloyed definitions. *This she was able to do because of her understanding of the great controversy between God and Satan.*

What is especially amazing is the internal harmony that pervades the five volumes of the Conflict of the Ages set. It could be compared to the emergence of an oak tree from its acorn. The acorn has within itself the characteristics and possibilities of the giant oak. The great controversy theme is God's acorn. All it needed were human beings who could and would recognize the amazing implications of this core truth about the universe—human beings who allowed themselves to be messengers of the Lord. Like the growth of the oak, the great controversy theme has unfolded step by step—first establishing stout, fundamental branches, and then building the smaller branches on the main ones.

God's side of the tree has the huge branch of His grace reaching out to supply that which earth's rebels need most—grace's double blessing of pardon and power—God's antidote for guilt and human powerlessness.

Man's side is the equally huge branch labeled "faith"—the habit of saying Yes to whatever God is asking for. That stout limb embraces appreciation, trust, joy, and willing obedience.

God's side continued to build branches. We call one of those glorious branches, Jesus—with smaller branches spreading out where we learn why He came to earth and why He died. Wonderful branches! Other branches develop, such as Christ's work as our High Priest in the heavenly sanctuary and how that New Testament truth connects with men and women in preparing them to live forever.

On our side, we develop branches that involve our understanding of human nature, that we were not created with immortal souls and that the wicked need not look forward to an eternally burning hell. We recognize that God created us with the power of reason and a will that gives us choices regarding right and wrong. We also recognize that sin happens when created beings say No to God and that all sinful choices involve consequences.

And so the tree grows, each branch spreading naturally. All because God planted that acorn in the soil called freedom—freedom to love or, unfortunately, not to love. The purpose—the glory—of this great controversy tree is the unfolding of God's wonderful character that always reaches out to His creation; He never holds back His love even when created beings disagree with Him or even when they revolt and try to run their lives according to their self-centered desires. The tree stands sturdy no matter how hard evil winds may blow. That tree depicting God's character in the great controversy is the universe's only guarantee that God's creation will be eternally secure.

In many ways God has revealed His character—the character that Satan misrepresented so skillfully that one-third of the angels believed his deceptive lies and that most of earth's inhabitants have bought into. Probably God's clearest presentation of His character and how He thinks about His creation was at Calvary. Watch Him die in Gethsemane and at Golgotha!

If ever there was a time when He had the right to set things straight as to who was right in the great controversy, it was when jeering men and women not only rejected Him but smothered Him with their hatred and cruelty. But He answered not a word. Even on the Cross, His cup of mercy and patience flowed over. He did not respond to the jeers that He should come down off the cross if He were who He said He was. He did not finally lash out with holy vengeance. The most He would do was weep: "How can I give you up, Ephraim? How can I hand you over, Israel?" (Hosea 11:8). To the end, He was the God who never changes, the Lord who is the same today, yesterday, and forever.

To tell the truth about this kind of a God is the purpose of the plan of salvation. And the purpose of the gospel is to teach men and women how to fit into this universe-wide plan to bring the controversy to a close.

To bring all these truths into sharp focus, God designed that in the last days He would speak through His messenger. That person was Ellen White. Her literary vehicle was the great controversy theme through which this rebel planet could see and hear the truth about God.

Without this theme revealed in the Conflict of the Ages volumes, Seventh-day Adventists would probably not have lasted fifty years— and if they did, they would have made no more of an impression on the world than our friends in the Seventh Day Baptist Church.

Without this theme, the world would not have a clear context for the messages of Jesus' soon return and what happens to a person when he or she dies. This theme provides a reason for Adventists to have a distinctive educational system or a distinctive health program. Without this theme, Adventists, if they still remained, would stumble into the future with less and less reason to exist in the twenty-first century.

Much of what we are as a people has come about due to our understanding of this theme given in the great controversy visions. They have given us God's side of the awful controversy that has put the entire universe in a holding pattern since our Lord's adversary embarked on his self-destructive venture.

Read the five volumes of the Conflict of the Ages set, seeing for the first time, all over again, that "surely the Lord God does nothing, unless He reveals His secret to His servants the prophets" (Amos 3:7). "Believe in the Lord your God, and you shall be established; believe His prophets, and you shall prosper" (2 Chronicles 20:20).

---

1. E. G. White, *Education*, 125 (see chap. 4, n. 33).

2. E. G. White, *Christ's Object Lessons*, 419, 420 (see chap.4, n. 27).

3. E. G. White, *Early Writings*, 13–17 (see chap. 2, n. 4).

4. *Life Sketches of Ellen G. White* (Mountain View, Calif.: Pacific Press® Publishing Association, 1915), 162.

5. Ibid.

6. Ibid., 163.

7. Ibid.

8. I found Arthur L. White's "Ellen G. White's Portrayal of the Great Controversy Story" in *Spirit of Prophecy*, 4:507–549 very helpful; I have included some of his details here.

9. E. G. White, *The Great Controversy*, xi, xii (see chap. 2, n. 10). The phrase, "in our own time" easily included the writings of Uriah Smith and John N. Andrews.

10. Ibid., vi, vii.

11. Ibid., 38, cf. 338.

12. Ibid., 42.

13. Ibid., 73.

14. Ibid., 256.

15. Ibid., 425.

16. Ibid., 488.

17. Ibid., 488, 489.

18. Ibid., 504.

19. E. G. White, *Patriarchs and Prophets*, 68 (see chap. 6, n. 45).

20. Ibid., 69.

21. E. G. White, *Selected Messages*, vol. 3, 117, 118 (see chap. 4, n. 14).

22. E. G. White, *The Desire of Ages*, 48, 49 (see chap. 4, n. 33).

23. Ibid., 24.

24. Ibid., 671.

25. Ibid.

26. Ibid., 759.

27. Ibid., 761.

28. *Notebook Leaflets from the Elmshaven Library*, vol. 2 (Payson, Ariz.: Leaves-Of-Autumn Books, 1985), 196.

29. E. G. White, *Selected Messages*, vol. 3, 123, 124.

30. W. C. White wrote regarding these few passages that might arouse unnecessary controversy: "Mother has often said: 'What I have written regarding the arrogance and the assumptions of the papacy, is true. Much historical evidence regarding these matters has been designedly destroyed; nevertheless, that the book may be of the greatest benefit to Catholics and others, and that needless controversies may be avoided, it is better to have all statements regarding the assumptions of the pope and the claims of the papacy stated so moderately as to be easily and clearly proved from accepted histories that are within the reach of our ministers and students.' "—*Selected Messages*, vol. 3, 463. The full letter can be obtained from the Ellen G. White Estate, Silver Spring, Maryland.

Chapter Eight

THE OVERPOWERING APPEAL—"CAN'T WE ALL GET ALONG?"

In the 1880s Ellen White became especially aware of the wave of contemporary religious revivals that were both spurious and dramatically "successful." She predicted that these spurious revivals, reflecting great interest in spiritual matters, would become increasingly attractive and wider in appeal in the end time. In fact, spurious and widespread religious interest would become a key component in Satan's plan to divert attention from God's last-day appeal to honest seekers for truth the world over.

First, Ellen White described those revivals that she had experienced in earlier years:

> They were characterized by solemn, earnest appeals to the sinner, by yearning compassion for the purchase of the blood of Christ. Men and women prayed and wrestled with God for the salvation of souls. The fruits of such revivals were seen in souls who shrank not at self-denial and sacrifice, but rejoiced that they were counted worthy to suffer reproach and trial for the sake of Christ. Men beheld a transformation in the lives of those who had professed the name of Jesus. The community was benefited by their influence.

They gathered with Christ, and sowed to the Spirit, to reap life everlasting.[1]

Change in the middle of the nineteenth century

Then she described the change that came in the middle of the nineteenth century: "But many of the revivals of modern times have presented a marked contrast to those manifestations of divine grace which in earlier days followed the labors of God's servants. It is true that a widespread interest is kindled, many profess conversion, and there are large accessions to the churches; nevertheless the results are not such as to warrant the belief that there has been a corresponding increase of real spiritual life. The light which flames up for a time soon dies out, leaving the darkness more dense than before."[2]

She analyzed the reasons why these "popular revivals" appealed so strongly—an analysis that would also describe the increasing crescendo of end-time religious revivals: "Popular revivals are too often carried by appeals to the imagination, by exciting the emotions, by gratifying the love for what is new and startling. Converts thus gained have little desire to listen to Bible truth, little interest in the testimony of prophets and apostles. Unless a religious service has something of a sensational character, it has no attractions for them. A message which appeals to unimpassioned reason awakens no response. The plain warnings of God's word, relating directly to their eternal interests, are unheeded."[3]

In a nutshell

I don't know anyone who has described better, in a nutshell, the contemporary megachurches, such as Saddleback, Lake Forest, California; Willow Creek, South Barrington, Illinois; Prestonwood Baptist Church, Plano, Texas; and the Crystal Cathedral, Garden Grove, California—and hundreds more that are their clones! I certainly am not impugning anyone's sincerity. For the most part, pastors of these megachurches believe they are preaching the gospel as they know it. And for the most part, the parishioners are finding these modern religious services to be much more appealing than the stale, ritualistic, traditional programs in their previous churches.

How precisely descriptive, however, are Ellen White's words: the quest for something "new and startling!" This is exactly where the religious world is today in this generation that is plagued with postmodernism wherein it is politically incorrect to be judgmental and where authority, in general, is passé. With no absolute truths to bow to, all the world has left today is an appeal to the emotions! Or in the words of Ellen White: "Unless a religious service has something of a sensational character, it has no attractions for them." She could have written these words yesterday!

And how surgically accurate and specific is her analysis of present-day "religious" fervor: "A message which appeals to unimpassioned reason awakens no response." This insight is a clear indictment of the sweeping tsunami of the "new spirituality" that is affecting almost every church today.

Ellen White then predicted how God's truth in the end time will stand up to this "tsunami":

> Notwithstanding the widespread declension of faith and piety, there are true followers of Christ in these churches. Before the final visitation of God's judgments upon the earth there will be among the people of the Lord such a revival of primitive godliness as has not been witnessed since apostolic times. The Spirit and power of God will be poured out upon His children. At that time many will separate themselves from those churches in which the love of this world has supplanted love for God and His word. Many, both of ministers and people, will gladly accept those great truths which God has caused to be proclaimed at this time to prepare a people for the Lord's second coming.[4]

Satan's strategy during God's last appeal

But what will be Satan's strategy during this time when God's Spirit and power will be especially evident? Ellen White continued,

> The enemy of souls desires to hinder this work; and *before the time* for such a movement shall come, he will endeavor to *prevent it by introducing a counterfeit.* In those churches which he can bring under his deceptive power he will make it appear that God's special blessing is poured out; there will be manifest what is thought to be great religious interest. Multitudes will exult that God is working marvelously for them, when the work is that of another spirit. Under a religious guise, Satan will seek to extend his influence over the Christian world.
>
> In many of the revivals which have occurred during the last half century, the same influences have been at work, to a greater or less degree, that will be manifest in the *more extensive movements of the future.* There is an emotional excitement, a mingling of the true with the false, that is well adapted to mislead.[5]

What are the basic components of Satan's counterfeit that will mislead people into thinking that God's special blessing is present in their meetings? The components include

- "emotional excitement, a mingling of the true with the false, that is well adapted to mislead."[6]
- "neglect [of] the testimony of the Bible ... [and] testing truths which require self-denial and renunciation of the world."[7]
- "a wrong conception of the character, the perpetuity, and the obligation of the divine law ... [resulting] in lowering the standard of piety in the church."[8]

- "many religious teachers [who] assert that Christ by His death abolished the law, and men are henceforth free from its requirements."[9]
- "the hope of salvation [which] is accepted without a radical change of heart or reformation of life."[10]
- "erroneous theories of sanctification . . . springing from neglect or rejection of the divine law, [and] have a prominent place in the religious movements of the day."[11]
- "the desire for an easy religion that requires no striving, no self-denial, no divorce from the follies of the world, [and which] has made the doctrine of faith, and faith only, popular doctrine."[12]
- the idea that "it is of no consequence what men believe."[13]
- "passages of Scripture separated from the context."[14]
- the belief "that Satan has no existence as a personal being."[15]
- keeping "the minds of men searching and conjecturing in regard to that which God has not made known and which He does not intend that we shall understand."[16]
- "the theory of eternal torment."[17]
- the idea "that all mankind will finally be saved. . . . Thus, the sinner can live in selfish pleasure, disregarding the requirements of God, and yet expect to be finally received into His favor."[18]
- "a counterfeit so closely resembling the truth that it deceives those who are willing to be deceived, who desire to shun the self-denial and sacrifice demanded by the truth."[19]
- "a weak sentimentalism, making little distinction between good and evil. God's justice, His denunciations of sin, the requirements of His holy law, are all kept out of sight."[20]
- "thousands [who] deify nature while they deny the God of nature."[21]
- "church members [who] love what the world loves and are ready to join with them, and Satan determines to unite them

in one body and thus strengthen his cause by sweeping all into the ranks of spiritualism."[22]

We are warned that "so closely will the counterfeit resemble the true that it will be impossible to distinguish between them except by the Holy Scriptures."[23] And Ellen White goes on to point out that "many claim that it matters not what one believes, if his life is only right. But the life is molded by the faith. If light and truth is within our reach, and we neglect to improve the privilege of hearing and seeing it, we virtually reject it; we are choosing darkness rather than light."[24]

Not everyone falling under the fog of last-day counterfeits will believe or be affected by all the earmarks of counterfeits listed above. That fact alone gives us caution as we review the emerging leaders in the new spirituality. But they all share common threads that Ellen White identified with in her amazing prophetic predictions.

Paul's warning

It is interesting, as we look at the religious world all around us today, to read again the apostle Paul's warning regarding earth's last days:

> In the last days perilous times will come: For men will be lovers of themselves . . . having a form of godliness but denying its power.
>
> For the time will come when they will not endure sound doctrine, but according to their own desires, because they have itching ears, they will heap up for themselves teachers; and they will turn their ears away from the truth, and be turned aside to fables (2 Timothy 3:1–5; 4:3, 4).

Paul is giving us a heads-up! The old veteran is *not* talking about what will be going on in Buddhism, Hinduism, or Islam. He is warning the Christian church that in the end time the gospel that turned the world upside down in the first century (see Acts 17:6) would become so watered down that the secret of its power would be muted.

In the last days, Christians will seek teachers and preachers who will focus on their "felt" needs, rather than on their "real" needs. They will want our Lord's name, but not His character. They will prefer to "feel" their religion rather than build reasons for their faith that was once delivered to the first-century loyalists (see Jude 3).

Let's take a look at what has been happening in Evangelical Protestantism during the past twenty years. One of the most remarkable occurrences has been the emergence of new types of worship services and the rapid rise of megachurches throughout the United States. A tsunami wave of books such as Rick Warren's *The Purpose-Driven Life* and Joel Osteen's *Your Best Life Now* are heralded around the world for their practical spiritual counsel, heavily buttressed with biblical texts. So what's the problem?

Something deeper is going on. In the first half of the twentieth century, the shift within Christianity was a retreat from its historical defense of the Bible's accuracy in the face of the attacks from modern liberalism. Today, the shift within Christianity is one of moving away from its traditional biblical base to a more psychological, sociological base, headed by the philosophies of pragmatism and new spirituality. Of course, the Bible is used, but often it is not only misquoted and mistranslated; it becomes a grab bag to support whatever concept the user chooses to promote.

That is the new twist. For more than a century, liberal Protestants jettisoned the Bible as a reliable spiritual authority. Today's Evangelicals, once the guardians of the authority of Scripture, do not deny the Bible itself. Instead, by the way they use it, they give the appearance that the Bible is not really all that important on certain points. It is only a short step, then, to looking to other sources of truth that seem more relevant, more personal, more satisfying than God's Word.

Seeking personal assurance

History seems to show that when those looking for authentic spirituality do not find it in churches where the authority of the Bible is upheld, they will seek elsewhere for some kind of personal assurance and authority. Few return to their traditional church services because they feel burned over with dry and irrelevant sermons, boring liturgies, and repetitive traditions. Such seekers, and there are many in *all* churches, still look for something that seems personally satisfying and that does not require that they change the language and feel of Christianity—and that is exactly what is happening. Many pastors, recognizing this spiritual desert, search for the next spiritual experience that will validate their ministries.

Newsweek (August 29, 2005) featured a cover story "In Search of the Spiritual." The subtitle was "Move over, politics. Americans are looking for personal, ecstatic experiences of God, and, according to our poll, they don't much care what the neighbors are doing."

The new spirituality emphasis has captured the attention and commitment of a great number of younger people. New spirituality promises contact with God in ways not experienced in more conventional Christian paths.

Spiritualism vs. spirituality

We must distinguish between age-old spiritualism and the emerging new spirituality. As we noted in chapter 5, spiritualism is the open appeal to find reality, God, cosmic consciousness, etc., through *direct* contact with the "other" world. Contact could be made through channeling, Ouija boards, séances, or certain kinds of extrasensory perception.

New spirituality, at this time, doesn't go in that direction, although it has much in common with spiritualism. Both concepts believe in either the immortal soul or the subjective ability to find God or reality within one's self through any number of modalities. Neither believes in the final authority of Scripture.

The modern mood in the twenty-first century

In his book *The Next American Spirituality*, pollster George Gallup writes that spirituality is very much alive in America today, but that it is without biblical foundation. "Contemporary spirituality can resemble a grab bag of random experiences that does little more than promise to make our eyes mist up or our heart warm. We need perspective to separate the junk food from the wholesome, the faddish from the truly transforming."[25]

The problem, as Gallup sees it, is the massive amount of biblical illiteracy among Christians generally throughout the world. "Half," he says, "of those describing themselves as Christians are unable to name who delivered the Sermon on the Mount. Many Americans cannot name the reason for celebrating Easter or what the Ten Commandments are. People think the name of Noah's wife was Joan, as in Joan of Ark."[26]

Then Gallup describes the "great disconnect"—the wide gulf between what Americans in general and Christians in particular *claim to believe* and how they *actually live*. He concludes that this "cluster of moral and theological shortcomings seemingly throws into question the transforming power of religious beliefs." He adds, "Just because Americans claim they are more spiritual does not make them so."[27] And then he asks the burning question, "Is the church really rediscovering its spiritual moorings, or just engaging in retreat from seemingly insoluble problems?"[28]

Filling the vacuum

Most people are spiritually hungry, and they will find some spiritual leader who promises to satisfy their search for meaning. Itching ears will find teachers to meet their desires (see 2 Timothy 4:3). That is why the new spirituality is sweeping over the American church. It comes in many forms. Based on the content of their Web sites and the books they endorse, many, if not most, of the megachurches are riding this wave, although they may not suspect its pending disaster in the end times.

Promoters of new spirituality are generally gracious, charming, and very believable in that they believe what they say and they believe that what they have experienced should be shared with the world. And much of what they say is indeed appealing, as proved by the sale of their books! The issue, however, is that new spirituality's focus and emphasis are light years removed from biblical teaching.

John MacArthur, well-known pastor and author in southern California, summed up this phenomenon like this: "The evangelical consensus has shifted decidedly in the past two decades. Our collective message is now short on doctrine and long on experience. Thinking is deemed less important than feeling. . . . The love of sound doctrine that has always been a distinguishing characteristic of evangelicalism has all but disappeared. Add a dose of mysticism to this mix, and you have the recipe for unmitigated spiritual disaster."[29]

The age of Aquarius

As we have discovered in the past forty years, the term New Age is synonymous with "The Age of Aquarius." The central teaching of each is that we are supposed to understand, one way or another, that God is within each person and can be found. The New Age movement that seemed so radical in the '60s and '70s did not die out. Rather, it integrated itself into society seemingly everywhere—medicine, business, schools, science, and finally even in the last frontier, the Evangelical church. Though the banner is no longer "New Age," its key elements have morphed in even greater degree into the pervasive new spirituality.[30]

This chapter is not an attempt to explain fully the New Age thought, but to point out how and through whom New Age concepts are creeping into the pulpits and seminaries of churches everywhere. New movements or changes within Christianity usually come with great leaders proclaiming new ways to look at the gospel. This was the case with the Reformation leaders and later with John Wesley. But New Age concepts have invaded the church quietly, like a cancer. Unnoticed at first, it gradually eats away faith and finally takes over the whole body unless it is recognized for what it is. Cancer treatment is not pleasant but necessary. Without treatment, the body eventually dies.

Many Evangelical churches first rejected New Age concepts but then gradually began to welcome certain aspects of its teachings. Over time, many Evangelical churches have unwittingly become the "New Age Church." Ears have been tickled. Most do not realize that they are full of cancer, but live on in bliss with their New Age anesthetic.

New spirituality feeders

M. Scott Peck. Author of one of the bestsellers of all time, *The Road Less Traveled*, Scott Peck has written a number of books that occupy a substantial share of bookstore shelf space in the self-help section. When *The Road Less Traveled* was first published, I was an instant admirer. (In fact, Peck's *People of the Lie*[31] is still the best book I have ever read about analyzing evil.) But when I reached his question "What does God want from us?" and then his answer, "It is for the individual to become totally, wholly God,"[32] I knew something troubling was happening, although at that time, I was unclear about his New Age journey.

Peck wrote in his book *A World Waiting to Be Born,*

> This process of emptying the mind is of such importance it will continue to be a significant theme. ... It may help to remember, therefore, that the purpose of emptying the mind is not ultimately to have nothing there; rather it is to make room in the mind for something new, something unexpected, to come in. What is the something new? It is the voice of God.[33]

He also writes that Jesus was "an example of the Western mystic [who] integrated himself with God," that Jesus' message to us was

"cease clinging to our lesser selves [and find] our greater true selves."
Contemplative prayer[34] "is a lifestyle dedicated to maximum awareness."[35]

Michael D'Antonio, a secular journalist, in his book *Heaven on Earth*,
wrote that he saw Peck as "the Billy Graham of the New Age . . . a major New Age leader."[36]

Thomas Merton. Merton (1915–1968) probably influenced New Age
spirituality more than any other person in the twentieth century. And
he's probably the individual most quoted by promoters of the new
spirituality. Roman Catholics highly praise Merton's works. One classic
reference sets forth Merton's core belief: "It is a glorious destiny to be a
member of the human race . . . now I realize what we all are. . . . If only
they [people] could all see themselves as they really are. . . . I suppose
the big problem would be that we would fall down and worship each
other. . . . At the center of our being is a point of nothingness which is
untouched by sin and by illusions, a point of pure truth. . . . It is in
everybody. This little point . . . is the pure glory of God in us."[37]

Henri Nouwen. A Dutch Catholic priest (1932–1996), Henri Nouwen
authored forty books on the spiritual life. A survey by *Christian Century* magazine, conducted in 2003, indicated that Nouwen's work was
a first choice for Catholic and mainline Protestant clergy.

Nouwen is praised for his warm, comforting appeal and impressive
piety. But he walked firmly on the path of new spirituality. Note his
endorsement of the use of a mantra,[38] a common thread in new spirituality: "The quiet repetition of a single word can help us to descend
with the mind into the heart. . . . This way of simple prayer . . . opens us
to God's active presence."[39] In *Bread for the Journey*, he wrote, "Prayer
is 'soul work' because our souls are those sacred centers where all is
one. . . . It is in the heart of God that we can come to the full realization
of the unity of all that is."[40]

Nouwen and Merton believed that their priestly experiences with
silence were something that Protestants should understand, that they

should get the blessing of silence, shorthand for contemplative prayer.

Thomas Keating and M. Basil Pennington. Keating and Pennington, two Catholic monks, have written a number of popular books on contemplative prayer, such as *Centered Living: The Way of Centering Prayer,* and *Open Mind, Open Heart.* In *Finding Grace at the Center,* they wrote, "We should not hesitate to take the fruit of the age-old wisdom of the East and 'capture' it for Christ. Indeed, those of us who are in ministry should make the necessary effort to acquaint ourselves with as many of these Eastern techniques as possible. . . . Many Christians who take their prayer life seriously have been greatly helped by Yoga, Zen, TM, and similar practices, especially where they have been initiated by reliable teachers and have a solidly developed Christian faith to find inner force and meaning to the resulting experiences."[41]

Pennington wrote, "The soul of the human family is the Holy Spirit."[42]

Gerald G. May. May (1940–2005), a psychiatrist, was known for his leadership in the Christian twelve-step field and for being a cofounder and teacher in the Shalem Prayer Institute in Washington, D.C. The Institute is a powerful leader in contemplative prayer. Admittedly strongly influenced by Eastern religions, May wrote in *Addiction and Grace* (acclaimed as a classic in addiction recovery) that "our core . . . one's center . . . is where we realize our essential unity with one another and with all God's creation." He then stated how this is achieved: "I am not speaking here of meditation that involves guided imagery or scriptural reflections, but of a more contemplative practice in which one just sits still and stays awake with God."[43] In *The Awakened Heart* he made it even clearer that he was in the mystical panentheistic[44] camp when he talked about "cosmic presence" as revealed in "the Hindu greetings of *jai bhagwan* and *namaste* that reverence the divinity that both resides within and embraces us all."[45]

John Main. A Benedictine monk (1926–1982), Main seems to be quoted by almost everyone involved in the new spirituality. He popularized contemplative prayer as the "way of the mantra" first taught to him by a Hindu monk.[46] In 1977, he and Laurence Freeman founded a monastery in Montreal dedicated to a revival of ancient prayer methods, chief of which is repeating a mantra. *Maranatha,* an Aramaic word that means "Come, Lord Jesus," is often chosen for their mantras. Freeman has continued the work that Main began and has founded the World Community for Christian Meditation.

Matthew Fox. Once a Catholic priest and now an Episcopalian, Fox has written more than two dozen books and developed an enormous following in Catholic and Protestant circles. He is a popular speaker, especially in New Age circles, emphasizing his panentheistic views.

Richard Foster. One of the most well-known people in the new spirituality movement, Foster founded Renovaré, an organization committed to working for the renewal of the Church of Jesus Christ. Renovaré holds regional and local conferences bringing together Christians across denominational lines. Foster's best-known books include *Celebration of Discipline* (hailed by *Christianity Today* as one of the ten best books of the twentieth century[47]), *Streams of Living Water, Freedom of Simplicity,* and *The Challenge of the Disciplined Life.*

Of course, Foster has much that is devotionally helpful. But it doesn't take long to realize that he advocates a prayer movement that has strong links to Eastern mysticism.[48] Contemplative prayer— saturated with New Age concepts, Eastern mysticism, universalism, and pantheism—is now infiltrating Christianity big time.

In addition to his own writings, Foster has a great proclivity to quote or endorse others who are closely linked to Buddhism, such as the Catholic mystic Thomas Merton, whom he quotes thirteen times in *Celebration of Discipline.* Merton wrote, "I think I couldn't understand Christian teaching the way I do if it were not in the light of Buddhism."[49]

In the back of *Celebration of Discipline*, Foster lists Tilden Edwards's book *Spiritual Friend*, as an "excellent book on spirituality." Edwards's position is well known. He has written, "This mystical stream [contemplative prayer] is the Western bridge to Far Eastern spirituality."[50]

The fascinating, as well as alarming, fact is that Foster and others wrap their particular goals and methodologies in biblical words so that average readers feel they are truly being blessed. In fact, many Evangelicals would be disturbed by the charge that Foster is promoting a pseudo-Christian mysticism.[51]

Most people only read superficially in Foster and don't think twice about what he says regarding visualization, one of the modalities he offers for finding "reality" within. He writes,

> You can actually encounter the living Christ in the event. It can be more than an exercise of the imagination, it can be a genuine confrontation. . . . Jesus Christ will actually come to you.[52]

> In your imagination allow your spiritual body, shining with light, to rise out of your physical body . . . up through the clouds into the stratosphere . . . deeper and deeper into outer space until there is nothing except the warm presence of the eternal Creator.[53]

He goes on to state that this is more than imagination; it is reality created with the mind.

Brennan Manning. This delightful ex-Catholic priest wrote *The Ragamuffin Gospel*, an emotionally gripping focus on God's forgiving nature and His love for the unworthy—but Manning works with a limited gospel. Like Foster, he has struck a responsive chord among Evangelicals who buy into his pleasing, passionate graciousness.

In his book *The Signature of Jesus*, Manning characterizes a contemplative spiritualist as one who "looks upon human nature as fallen but *redeemed*, flawed but in essence good."[54] He wrote, "The first step in faith is to stop thinking about God at the time of prayer."[55] The second step is "without moving your lips, repeat the sacred word [or phrase] inwardly, slowly, and often." If distractions come, "simply return to listening to your sacred word."[56] He also encourages his readers to "celebrate the darkness" because "the ego has to break; and this breaking is like entering into a great darkness."[57]

Manning strongly recommends Basil Pennington's book *Centering Prayer*, saying that Pennington's methods provide "a way of praying that leads to a deep living relationship with God."[58]

Other best-selling new spirituality authors

Leonard Sweet's[59] book *SoulTsunami* is filled with positive quotes and material from New Agers and globalists such as James Redfield, author of *The Celestine Prophecy*; Sarah Ban Breathnach; Annie Dillard; Tom Sine; Wayne Dyer; and countless other well-known mystics and/or New Agers. This passage from Sweet's book *Quantum Spirituality* is common to new spirituality ideas: "If I find Christ, I will find my true self and if I find my true self, I will find Christ."[60]

Sincere Christians should pause and ask three questions:

1. In their rejection of dry sermons and stale church programs, should Christians run from basic biblical principles and embrace cutting-edge, exotic new spirituality just because it couches its language in Christian terms, promising a fresh devotional life?

2. Should Christians allow the appeal of instant gratification that permeates modern living govern their spiritual connection with the God of the Bible—a very personal Father, Son, and Holy Spirit? Lasting friendships with people take time to nurture, to learn all one can about the other. New spirituality promises a new kind of "instant" gratification in the mantras of contemplative prayers.

3. Should Christians fall for what "works"? This pragmatic approach

has been a phenomenal shift of the last century, not only in politics or science but also in the religious world. The Christian world once believed, generally, that truth is determined by what God has said and not on what seems to work "for me." The test of truth should not be, Will it make me feel good about myself? New spirituality promises a self-actualized, self-fulfilling union with God that is nowhere recommended in the Bible.

Biblical "endorsement"

Psalm 46:10—"Be still and know that I am God"—is frequently used to promote "listening" or contemplative prayer. The DVD titled *Be Still* actually bears the inscription of Psalm 46:10 on its case.[61]

But as one should for any text, it is necessary to read the whole psalm. In this text, David is surely not recommending that we empty our minds from thought or words of any kind. Notice how the psalm begins: "God is our refuge and strength, a very present help in trouble." Or look at verse 8: "Come, behold the works of the Lord." Ignoring context is dangerous.

Christian colleges and seminaries promoting contemplative and emerging spirituality

For those of us who have known these college and seminaries a few decades ago, all this is mind-boggling. This list of educational institutions promoting these concepts of the new spirituality includes Assemblies of God Theological Seminary, Biola University, Canadian Mennonite University, George Fox University Seminary, Mars Hill Graduate School, Simpson University, Trinity Western University, and Wheaton College Graduate School. For example, at Assemblies of God Theological Seminary, the program is led by Earl Creps, whose syllabi include materials from Henri Nouwen, Brian McLaren, Ken Blanchard, Dan Kimball, Sally Morgenthaler, and Leonard Sweet.

An intriguing book

One of the most intriguing books published only days after September 11, 2001, is *From the Ashes—A Spiritual Response to the Attack on America*.[62] In the introduction, Steven Waldman wrote, "At times like this, we can all benefit from hearing a wide variety of voices. That is why we at Beliefnet, the leading multifaith Web site on religion and spirituality, teamed up with Rodale, Inc., to collect the most eloquent and wise voices across the faith spectrum."[63]

One of those "eloquent and wise voices" is Neale Donald Walsch, who wrote,

> The Bible, which is only one of humanity's many sources of spiritual teaching, carries this message throughout, in both the Old Testament and the New. (Have we not all one father? Has not one God created us? Why then are we faithless to one another, profaning the covenant of our fathers?—Malachi 2:10. . . . So we, though many, are one body in Christ, and individually members one of another,—Romans 12:5. . . . Because there is one bread, we who are many are one body—1 Corinthians 10:17).
>
> This is a message the human race has largely ignored. . . . We must change ourselves. We must change the beliefs upon which our behaviors are based. We must create a different reality, build a new society. And we must do so not with political truths or with economic trusts, and not with cultural truths or even the remembered truths of our ancestors—for the sins of the fathers are being visited upon the sons. We must do with new spiritual truths. We must preach a new gospel, its healing message summarized in two sentences:
>
> *We are all one.*
>
> *Ours is not a better way, ours is merely another way.*
>
> This fifteen-word message, delivered from every lectern and

pulpit, from every rostrum and platform, could change everything overnight.[64]

One of the Alliance's co-founders and member of its board of directors, Marianne Williamson, presented these New Age ideas on *The Oprah Winfrey Show* shortly after September 11. She outlined a peace plan based on New Age principles that would be an "alternative to Armageddon." And she announced Walsch would soon be presenting his Five-Step Peace Plan.

Explosion of peace plans

What shall we make of all this and much more? Since September 11, 2001, this planet has seen an enormous explosion of peace plans based on a new gospel that is touted as the only way to a true and lasting peace. And these plans are not mere wishes.

Let's be unequivocally clear: All of us seek peace. All of us want poverty, ignorance, and disease to be banished from this planet. Our challenge comes down to one question: What is the gospel message that permeates these various humanitarian uplift plans?

Modern peace plans are magnificently organized and enchantingly deceptive. What better way could be devised to set up the world with a unified voice that would heap ridicule on any group that would try to expose their errors? Never before has the whole world been wired and connected as today—Web-based computer systems, global cell-phone networks, international air travel, GPS systems, etc. A united voice, one mind, would speak, and immediately the whole world would see and hear![65]

Labyrinth

Another remarkable signal of new spirituality is the "labyrinth"[66] that is being featured at many Evangelical conferences, especially where younger members are being attracted. Often called "Amaze-ing Prayer," the labyrinth feature seems to fill the hunger of those who turn from well-choreographed worship services, every minute filled with music, videos, and preaching. Walking the "labyrinth" offers a private, unhurried, mystery-filled, meditative experience.

It seems that hungry experience-seekers are like moths drawn to the flame, ever seeking to know "god" through some kind of spiritual experience. Something seems to click in this pursuit. If you were handed a Ouija board and told that it had been totally redeemed by your spiritual leader and that it would bring you into a greater experience of God, would you use the occult device looking for the promised higher spiritual experience? Deuteronomy 12:1–4 and Exodus 34:10–17 admonish us not to use anything connected to pagan ritual. No question about it—such pagan gateways do lead to "spiritual" experiences of one's self and "god"—but it is the portal to the demonic.

At the National Pastors Conference in San Diego, March 9–13, 2004, the labyrinth path was formed by black lines on a thirty-foot-square piece of canvas laid on the floor. Participants were given a CD player with headphones to guide their journey through the eleven stations on the passageway. They were told not to rush but to slow down, breathe deeply, and fully focus on God.

Later in 2004, Graceland services at Santa Cruz Bible Church in California featured the labyrinth as part of its annual art event and sold "The Prayer Path" kit that transformed a room into a medieval prayer sanctuary. Leaders who promote these labyrinths rejoice that meditative prayer "resonates with hearts of emerging generations."

When I noticed that Zondervan Publishing Company, a leading new spirituality publisher, sponsored the National Pastor's Convention on February 22–25, 2006, I wondered who else is publishing new spirituality materials. To my surprise, I discovered that InterVarsity Press, NavPress (Navigators), Multnomah Books, Integrity, Thomas

Nelson, Bethany House, Harold Shaw, and HarperSanFrancisco all publish such materials. If I listed all the books now available, most readers would be equally shocked—they are the up-front, bestsellers wherever Christian books are sold!

What are the chief distinguishing characteristics of the new spirituality? Obviously, not every promoter of new spirituality emphasizes each of these characteristics, but it is easy to identify its promoters. The following are marks of the new spirituality:

- Functional denial of the authority of Scripture.
- Feelings eclipse reason in seeking truth.
- Contemplative, repetitive prayers.
- Visualizations to discover inner power and guidance.
- Abundant references to Roman Catholic mystics.
- Ancient "disciplines" are to be recovered and celebrated.
- Unmediated link to the absolute—"god" is within everyone.
- All paths lead to God.
- Finding one's core—the great mystery called "god."

Insider terms used by contemplatives

Like most experts in any field, contemplatives also use "inside" language that is clear to the initiated but means little to outsiders. For instance, you can track this "inside" language by noting the following terms and phrases—all of which have special meaning to those in the new spirituality movement:

spiritual formation, spiritual disciplines, beyond words, being in the present moment, slow prayer, awareness of being, mantra, inner light, divine center, practicing the presence, dark night of the soul, centering, centering prayer, ignation contemplation, spiritual direction, divine mystery, a thin place, ancient prayer practices, yoga, palms up/palms down, *lectio divina*, the

Jesus prayer, Jesus candles, breath prayers, prayer stations, en-
neagrams,[67] labyrinths.

Emergent church movement

Another feature of new spiritualism, but using a different approach, is the "emergent church" movement that has caught fire
within the last ten years. It is a reaction against various forms of Evangelicalism with their church-structured programs. Those in the emergent church movement find common ground with those who are doing their spiritual searching in local bars, cafés, and other leisure
centers. In other words, they are repotting Christianity in new cultural
and intellectual ground.

Some of these groups seem to emphasize being simple followers of
Jesus, avoiding the congregational milieu. They tend to be suspicious
of church hierarchy and doctrinal formulations; they talk of "emerging
authority." They are less concerned about safeguarding church bound-
aries; they use terms such as "liquid" churches. And they are much more
open to a wider sphere of activity than just evangelism.

One of the key "inside" terms is "cross over to the other side," or
variations of these words. Brian McLaren emphasizes this concept in
his book *The Church on the Other Side*.[68] Many use this term to depict a
radical break with historical Evangelical thought and practice. McLaren
goes beyond promoting a change in pastoral methods as a way of
dealing with the postmodern world. He challenges ministers to re-
think their message, not just their methods.[69]

Postmoderns, especially those in the emergent church movement, now insist that truth is no longer found in the objective teachings of the Bible but whatever the individual or community believes
it is; truth is whatever is arrived at through consensus. In other words,
contradiction with historical Christianity is not only acceptable, it is
welcomed. However one says it, "crossing over to the other side"
means an upfront denial of the New Testament gospel. If Jude was

moved to warn believers in his day, "I found it necessary to write to you exhorting you to contend earnestly for the faith which was once for all delivered to the saints" (Jude 3), one wonders what he would say today.

The emergent church movement is not a fad; it will find common ground across all denominational lines, especially among the young who search for new ways to express themselves in spiritual pursuits.

Marks of the emergent church movement

- The Bible is no longer the ultimate authority for many well-known leaders.
- The Bible is dumbed-down with emphasis placed on images and sensual experiences.
- Emphasis is placed on "what's in it for me" in the "here and now."
- More emphasis is given to the kingdom of God on earth than to Christ's return.
- Many bridges are established that lead to unity with the Roman Catholic Church.
- A belief that Christianity needs to be re-invented to provide "meaning" for this generation.
- A trend toward ecumenical unity for world peace, with emphasis on many ways to find God.

Counterfeiting the everlasting gospel

What does the new spirituality have to do with "counterfeits" in the end time? Ellen White wrote, "Satan can present a counterfeit so closely resembling the truth that it deceives those who are willing to be deceived, who desire to shun the self-denial and sacrifice demanded by the truth; but it is impossible for him to hold under his power one soul who honestly desires, at whatever cost, to know the truth."[70]

Ellen White accurately exposed this counterfeit gospel as she observed it developing in her day with its new cloak:

There is a spurious experience prevailing everywhere. Many are continually saying, "All that we have to do is to believe in Christ." They claim that faith is all we need. In its fullest sense, this is true; but they do not take it in the fullest sense. To believe in Jesus is to take him as our redeemer and our pattern. If we abide in him and he abides in us, we are partakers of his divine nature, and are doers of his word. The love of Jesus in the heart will lead to obedience to all his commandments. But the love that goes no farther than the lips is a delusion; it will not save any soul. Many reject the truths of the Bible, while they profess great love for Jesus; but the apostle John declares, "He that saith, I know him, and keepeth not his commandments, is a liar, and the truth is not in him." While Jesus has done all in the way of merit, we ourselves have something to do in the way of complying with the conditions. "If ye love me," said our Saviour, "keep my commandments."[71]

Ellen White predicted that a counterfeit gospel would become a worldwide movement capturing the attention and praise of the media. A counterfeit gospel is always a limited gospel, a gospel of convenience that will satisfy modern "felt" needs. The consequence of a counterfeit, limited gospel so prevalent today, especially in the seeker-friendly churches, is a church full of people enjoying the grace of forgiveness but with no clear grasp of the grace of power that will indeed make them into overcomers.

One of the chief reasons for this limited understanding of the grace of power (see Hebrews 4:16) is a cloudy understanding of why the commandments of God are essential to salvation. A related reason for the appeal of these various versions of a limited gospel is the separation of Christ as our Sacrifice and Christ as our High Priest. In short, this separation destroys the linkage between the grace of pardon and the grace of power and results in a focus on the gift of forgiveness without likewise recognizing the gift of transformation that prepares people for living eternally in a universe once again free from rebellion.

Summary

In the last twenty-five years, a spiritual tsunami known as new spirituality has been sweeping over North America. Much of the noted increase in spirituality across denominational lines as well as the experience of those who have bolted from their former denominational ties is centered in finding meaning in life through personal, subjective feeling. General bookstores, as well as Christian markets, are awash with bestsellers that promote finding reality within through contemplative prayer, walking labyrinths, and imaging the fulfillment of promises made by prosperity preachers.

Turned off by conventional churches that have lost their spiritual pulse, these followers of the new spirituality also have turned away from the Bible as a source of divine revelation. But these turned-off ones are not leaving the circle of Christianity to follow the occult world; without realizing it, they are helping the occult world remodel the Christian church. When clear Bible texts are made to say that "God is in everything, and everything is in God," we should recognize the subtle deception that is flooding even Christian bookstores.

Never has a generation of young and old, of rich and poor, thrown themselves so headlong into the winds of subjectivism, hoping to satisfy their desires for spiritual warmth without self-denial. The world on all continents is being led to conform to a universal spirituality that proclaims the oneness of all, a brotherhood of believers who live in tolerance toward one another's religious beliefs because the "reality" they worship is deeper than divisive doctrine. This global, unifying spirituality positions the world to welcome the great impersonator—

Satan himself—when he imitates the return of Jesus.

Last-day appeals of "Can't we all get along?" will be more than in-timidating; they will be coercive, leading to the day when men and women who don't go along will not be able to buy or sell. In fact, they will be condemned to be killed for their defense of truth (see Revelation 13:15, 17).

What I find to be more than astonishing is the accuracy, the unam-biguous warning that Ellen White has provided willing loyalists in the end time who have learned to trust her divine messages.

"Believe in the Lord your God, and you shall be established; believe His prophets, and you shall prosper" (2 Chronicles 20:20).

1. E. G. White, *The Great Controversy*, 462 (see chap. 2, n. 10).
2. Ibid., 463.
3. Ibid.
4. Ibid., 464.
5. Ibid. (emphasis supplied).
6. Ibid.
7. Ibid.
8. Ibid., 465.
9. Ibid., 466.
10. Ibid., 468.
11. Ibid., 469.
12. Ibid., 472,
13. Ibid., 520.
14. Ibid., 521.
15. Ibid., 524.
16. Ibid., 523.
17. Ibid., 536.
18. Ibid., 537.
19. Ibid., 528.
20. Ibid., 558.
21. Ibid., 583.
22. Ibid., 588.
23. Ibid., 593.
24. Ibid., 597.
25. (Colorado Springs: ChariotVictor, 2000), 15.

26. Ibid., 30.

27. Ibid., 32, 29.

28. Ibid.

29. *Reckless Faith* (Wheaton, Ill.: Crossway Books, 1994), 154, 155.

30. One of the most lucid books on how new spirituality is changing the face of Christianity is Ray Yungen's *A Time of Departing* (Silverton, Ore.: Lighthouse Trails Publishing Company, 2002).

31. (New York: Simon & Schuster, 1983).

32. (New York: Simon & Schuster, 1978), 283.

33. (New York: Bantam Books, 1993), 88, 89.

34. Contemplative prayer is not biblical prayer, no matter how spiritual it sounds. Rather, it is turning off our minds—putting them into neutral, in order to experience "the silence." Throwing our mind out of gear and trusting God to fill it not only has no biblical warrant but is an open door to spiritual deception. Paul said, "I will pray with the spirit, and I will also pray with the understanding" (1 Corinthians 14:15).

35. Peck, *A World Waiting to Be Born*, 83.

36. (New York: Crown Publishing, 1992), 342, 352.

37. *Conjectures of a Guilty Bystander* (Garden City, N.Y.: Doubleday, 1966), 140ff.

38. Mantra, as used in Eastern religions and New Age thought, means a repeated word or phrase. The basic process is to focus and maintain concentration without thinking about what one is thinking about. Conscious thinking is gradually tuned out until an altered state of consciousness is achieved.

39. *The Way of the Heart* (San Francisco: HarperSanFrancisco, 1981), 81.

40. (San Francisco: HarperSanFrancisco, 1996), January 15, November 16.

41. (Petersham, Mass.: St. Bede's Publications, 1978), 5, 6.

42. *Centered Living: The Way of Centering Prayer* (New York: Doubleday, 1986), 104.

43. (San Francisco: Harper and Row, 1988), 102, 166.

44. Panentheism combines the classic theism (a personal God) with pantheism (God is impersonal, pervading all creation). Panentheism is the foundational worldview of those engaged in mystical, contemplative prayer—God's presence in all things. That is why so many new spirituality leaders talk about "all is one."

45. (San Francisco: HarperSanFrancisco, 1991), 179.

46. "Lives of the Heart and Soul," *Maclean's* magazine, September 17, 1987, 42.

47. *Christianity Today*, April 24, 2000.

48. "Every distraction of the body, mind, and spirit must be put into a kind of suspended animation before this deep work of God upon the soul can occur." *Celebration of Discipline* (San Francisco: HarperSanFrancisco, 1978 edition), 13.

49. Frank X. Tuoti, *The Dawn of the Mystical Age* (New York: Crossroad Publishing Co., 1997), 127.

50. *Spiritual Friend* (New York: Paulist Press, 1979), 18.

51. In *Christianity Today*, October 2005, Richard J. Foster and Dallas Willard were interviewed in "The Making of the Christian." If one read only this article, he or she would have no idea what kind of philosophies and methodologies for which these two gracious men are known. It shows again that most anyone can be received with open arms if only he continues to use conventional Christian terms in promoting his core message, even if that message does not begin with the authority of the Bible.

52. *Celebration of Discipline* (San Francisco: Harper, 1988 edition), 26.

53. Ibid., 27.

54. *The Signature of Jesus* (Sisters, Ore.: Multnomah, 1996), 125.

55. Ibid., 212.

56. Ibid., 218.

57. Ibid., 145.

58. Back cover, *The Ragamuffin Gospel* (Sisters, Ore.: Multnomah Press, 1990).

59. Endorsement on the cover of Sweet's book, *SoulTsunami* (Grand Rapids: Zondervan, 2001). "*SoulTsunami* shows us why these are the greatest days for evangelism since the first century." Sweet is well known for his focus on unity—a worldwide oneness reflected in the growing union between the East and the West. In Sweet's *Quantum Spirituality* (Dayton, Ohio: United Theological Seminary, 1991), we read, "Energy-fire experiences take us into ourselves only that we might reach outside of ourselves. Metanoia is a de-centering experience of connectedness and community." "The power of small groups is in their ability to develop the discipline to get people 'in-phase' with the Christ consciousness and connected with one another."—147.

60. Ibid., 125.

61. April 2006, Fox Home Entertainment released the *Be Still* DVD, featuring Richard Foster, Dallas Willard, Calvin Miller, and Beth Moore—all with one main message: You cannot know God if you do not practice the art of going into the silence. That silence is not normal prayer, talking to a personal God, but a special state of mind induced through contemplative prayer that helps "believers" to avoid the addiction to use words.

62. (Emmaus, Pa.: Rodale Press, 2001).

63. Ibid., ix.

64. Ibid., 19–21.

65. See chapter 3.

66. The labyrinth is a path usually designed with intricate passageways and blind alleys. The most famous labyrinth of ancient times was the Cretan lair of the mythological Minotaur. Turf labyrinths still exist in England, Germany, and Scandinavia and were linked to fertility rituals. The Roman Catholic Church adopted the practice, and Christians made their pilgrimages to cathedrals in Chartres, Rheims, or Amiens where they completed their spiritual journeys in the cathedral

labyrinths. The patterns of the labyrinth are similar to Buddhist mandalas and the Japanese Zen practice of *kinhin* "walking meditation." Jean Houston, in the early 1990s, introduced the Christian world again to the practice of seeking enlightenment through walking the labyrinth when she linked up with Lauren Artress, spiritual leader of Grace Cathedral in San Francisco, to bring people back to their center and allow them to experience "Spirit" for themselves. See http://www .gracecathedral.org/labyrinth/. Jean Houston is listed on the Internet as one of the top ten New Age speakers in North America. Many participants at Gorbachev's State of the World Forum in 1997 also walked the labyrinth at Grace Cathedral.

67. The enneagram (or enneagon) is a nine-pointed geometric figure that is used in a number of teaching systems. The figure is believed to indicate the dynamic ways that certain aspects of things and processes are connected and change.

68. (Grand Rapids, Mich.: Zondervan, 2001).

69. Os Guinness said it well: "What happens . . . is drastic. Truths or customs that do not fit in with the modern assumption are put up in the creedal attic to collect dust. They are of no more use. The modification or removal of offending assumptions is permanent. What begins as a question of tactics escalates to a question of truth; apparently, the modern assumptions are authoritative. Is the traditional idea unfashionable, superfluous, or just plain wrong? No matter. It doesn't fit in, so it has to go."—*Prophetic Untimeliness: A Challenge to the Idol of Relevance* (Grand Rapids, Mich.: Baker Book House, 2003), 58.

70. E. G. White, *The Great Controversy*, 528.

71. *Historical Sketches of the Foreign Missions of the Seventh-day Adventists* (1886), 188, 189; see E. G. White, *The Great Controversy*, 464, 465.

HERE ARE MORE BOOKS BY DR. HERBERT EDGAR DOUGLASS
YOU WILL WANT TO HAVE IN YOUR PERSONAL LIBRARY.

Messenger of the Lord

God called a seventeen-year-old girl, frail and in poor health, to proclaim His Word and guide His people. For the next seventy years, Ellen White served as the Lord's messenger—writing, preaching, counseling, traveling, warning, and encouraging—as she faithfully delivered the communications God gave her for His church and the world.

Messenger of the Lord is the definitive work and the most comprehensive treatment ever produced of Ellen White's prophetic ministry.
Hardcover, 640 pages.   0-8163-1622-8   US$24.99

Also available in Spanish! *Mensajera del Señor (Messenger of the Lord)*
Hardcover, 590 pages.   (Distributed by Pacific Press®) 9-5057-3771-8   US$24.99

They Were There

They were there. They saw Ellen White and heard her speak. Why do their stories matter to us today? Each of the individuals involved in these stories was directly affected by Ellen White and her visions. They were there and saw for themselves the power of God that accompanied her work. Some continued to resist, but, for many, the result was a mighty confirmation of their faith in her life and ministry.
Paperback, 128 pages.   0-8163-2117-5   US$11.99

Truth Matters

The phenomenal success of the book *The Purpose-Driven Life*, by Rick Warren, has amazed Christians not only in America but around the world. Douglass readily acknowledges there is much value in Warren's book and in no way questions Warren's motives or his sincerity. Douglass's purpose in writing this book is threefold: to invite Adventists to take a second look at the theological direction of the movement, to urge those who have seen some of the dangers in the movement to recognize that many around the world have found spiritual nourishment in the program, and to urge all to recognize basic error is defeated, not by heated arguments, but by quiet truth.
Paperback, 224 pages.   0-8163-2156-6   US$15.99

Order from your ABC by calling **1-800-765-6955**, or get online and shop our virtual store at **http://www.AdventistBookCenter.com**.
• Read a chapter from your favorite book
• Order online
• Sign up for e-mail notices on new products

Prices subject to change without notice.